Praise for
Feeling the Flow
Creating Freedom from Shy Bladder Syndrome

"Having just completed Michael Hurd's *Feeling the Flow*, I am deeply impressed by this luminous addition to the literature on shy bladder syndrome, also known as paruresis. With remarkable candor and eloquence, Michael shares his transformative journey of recovery, illuminating the path for others with wisdom and hope. His narrative is both insightful and profoundly moving, offering not just practical guidance but genuine inspiration. This book stands as an outstanding testament to resilience and the power of personal triumph."

~ **Steven Soifer,** Ph.D., M.S.W., Advisor and Consultant, International Paruresis Association, co-author of *The Secret Social Phobia: Shy Bladder Syndrome (Paruresis)*, Treasurer, American Restroom Association, Adjunct Professor, Adelphi University School of Social Work

"In *Feeling the Flow*, Michael Hurd gives the paruresis community and its allies the gift of a clear, well-annotated, and honest memoir of his experiences of first struggling with, and then accepting and growing through his all-too-human confrontation with a limitation.

"Michael's progress, which he lays out in detail, is multi-modal, incorporating learnings from the fields of coaching, applied psychology and philosophy. The reader follows him as a humble and admirable guide, who speaks plainly to the lived experience of anxiety and recovery.

"For the reader with paruresis, we feel seen as our reality is validated and echoed; we are truly not alone. The analogies to other struggles are also made evident, and all readers will feel a resonance to some issue with which they have struggled. He offers an escape route to the trap of conflating thought and reality, and points to the tools he has used to free himself, which can be useful to all.

"*Feeling the Flow* is a timely, helpful and meaningful addition to the growing body of literature and media around paruresis. I highly recommend Hurd's generous contribution to those with, or in relationship to, those with paruresis."

~ **Dan Rocker,** LCSW, MA, President, International Paruresis Association

"Reading *Feeling the Flow* by Michael Hurd felt like encountering a lifeline—one I wish had been available when I was younger. As someone who has lived with paruresis (shy bladder syndrome) for my entire life, I rarely come across a resource that so deeply understands the psychological and emotional toll this condition takes. Hurd not only captures the day-to-day struggles of those of us who live in the shadows of bathroom anxiety, but he also offers a powerful message of recovery rooted in honesty, self-awareness, and hope.

"What makes this book extraordinary for me is the integration of the Three Principles—Mind, Consciousness, and Thought—into the journey of healing from paruresis. I discovered these principles in 2016, and they've profoundly changed the way I relate to my thoughts and experiences. To see them so thoughtfully woven into a recovery narrative for a condition I've silently battled for decades is truly remarkable. The combination of these two life-shaping topics felt like a conversation I had been waiting for for a long time.

"Meeting the author, Mike, at a paruresis workshop only deepened my appreciation for his story. His openness, vulnerability and courage in sharing decades of shame, coping strategies, and eventual healing are not only brave—they're transformative. Through his narrative, I saw echoes of my own life: the avoidance, the shame, the overthinking, and the desperate wish to be 'normal.' His story gave me the strength to step into my authenticity and continue on the path of healing.

"Mike's description of public restrooms as Mount Everest challenges rang painfully true. But his account of gradual victories—voiding at a urinal, using an airplane bathroom, or simply not overthinking every outing—made me believe recovery is possible. The practical techniques he shares, including graduated exposure and breath holding, are grounded in real-world applications and personal experience rather than abstract theory. Just as impactful is his philosophical insight that our thoughts are not facts, and that we suffer when we unknowingly give them power.

"At fifty-nine years old, I couldn't help but reflect on how much easier some of my earlier years might have been if a book like this had been available. The teenage and young adult years can be especially isolating when dealing with paruresis, and this book could be a lifeline for anyone, especially men and women navigating identity, relationships, and self-worth during those tender stages of life.

"In the end, *Feeling the Flow* is far more than a book about a bladder condition. It's a testimony to human courage, self-compassion, and the power of insight. It's a call to stop hiding and start healing. I wholeheartedly recommend it not just for those with paruresis but for anyone seeking freedom from invisible struggles and a deeper understanding of their own mind."

~ **Michael Lehrman,** Co-Publisher, *Natural Awakenings*—NYC & Long Island Editions, NaturalAwakeningsNY.com

"*Feeling the Flow* by Michael Hurd is one of the first books written from the perspective of someone who lives with paruresis, commonly known as shy bladder syndrome, and not by a medical professional. This makes it a refreshingly honest and deeply personal account of what it truly feels like to struggle with this condition.

"Hurd shares his lifelong journey with paruresis, detailing the emotional and psychological toll it took, and ultimately how he found a way to manage and overcome it. For most of his life, he believed he was alone in his suffering. But through a process of calming his thoughts and surrendering to the flow of the Universe, he came to realize that this condition is far more common than he imagined, affecting people all over the world.

"The turning point came in 2023, after a traumatic cross-country flight and a distressing experience in an airplane lavatory. Feeling desperate, he asked the Universe for help, and an answer appeared. He listened, he accepted and he said yes.

"This book chronicles his transformation from someone who couldn't urinate in a public bathroom to someone who now does so freely and without fear. His story is not just about recovery, but about finding peace, self-compassion, and even joy. He no longer lives in shame and isolation. He lives in love and hope.

"By the end of the book, Hurd even likens using a public restroom to playing a game, one filled with new possibilities and, surprisingly, even fun.

"If you are one of the many people silently living with paruresis, I wholeheartedly encourage you to read this book. Michael's journey is inspiring, relatable, and ultimately uplifting."

~ **Steven Weinraub,** International Paruresis Association Board Member and Support Group Co-Leader

"Mike has written a hopeful, helpful, hard-to-classify book, and I'm grateful to him for it. It's a memoir, told with vulnerability and clarity. It's a shy bladder manual, full of resources and insights for those struggling with paruresis. Most importantly, it's an exploration of how our thinking shapes our reality, and our mind-boggling power to change our lives for the better. If you have a shy bladder, this book is definitely for you. If you don't have a shy bladder, this book is still for you."

~ **Steven Jackson,** Director (*Pee Shy*)

"Michael Hurd's new book, *Feeling the Flow*, is really three books in one: it is a chronicle of his lonely struggle with paruresis, it is a narrative of his recent discovery of the International Paruresis Association and his remarkable progress toward recovery from the disorder, and it is an introspective guide through the life-lessons that he has learned along the way. Mike's conversational style is engaging, forthright and honest, and while he provides a great deal of valuable information about all aspects of the disorder itself and the recovery process, it is his personal journey which is the thread throughout the book, and it is truly inspiring. I would encourage anyone suffering from paruresis to read this book; it may just change your life."

~ **David Kliss,** International Paruresis Association (IPA) Board Member and Support Group Leader

"While *Feeling the Flow* is framed around the experience of 'shy bladder,' its insights extend far beyond that specific challenge. Michael Hurd offers profound and clear insight into how our thoughts can control us and how breaking free from the stories we tell ourselves can transform our lives. As he writes, 'The power of thought provides every human being the gift of being able to create our reality, whatever that reality is to us in the moment.'

"Hurd's honest and thoughtful exploration reveals that 'our lives can change in a moment just by changing our minds,' a hopeful and empowering message that resonates deeply. His writing provides a meaningful peek into the human condition, reminding us that 'you never know what another person is experiencing.'

"This inspirational and thought-provoking work encourages self-awareness, compassion, and emotional freedom, making it a valuable resource for anyone interested in personal growth and mental well-being. Ultimately, *Feeling the Flow* invites readers to embrace the power within themselves to create a more mindful and fulfilling reality."

~ **Dr. Holly J. Brown,** DAOM, LAc

"This book will be a godsend for anyone suffering with this under-recognized shy bladder syndrome. Michael's journey is your journey—not so much in the details as in the ups and downs of dealing with this condition. You will find that his answer will become your answer as well.

"If you have been struggling in quiet desperation, this book will start you on the road to 'feeling the flow' in more ways than one!"

~ **Catherine Casey,** BSW, MS Clinical Psychology, International Three Principles Consultant

"*Feeling the Flow* is a beautiful invitation to see that what we feel most up against in life might actually be the doorway to something deeper and freer, and to a life that feels full of meaning. Mike's journey of overcoming a fifty-year phobia is deeply personal, and yet it's about all of us.

"With compassion, humor and total honesty, he opens the possibility that freedom is not only available—it's closer than we think. Whether we struggle with paruresis, anxiety, depression, or any invisible weight we quietly carry, this book reminds us we're not alone.

"Mike doesn't just offer a formula; he offers something better: hope. Hope that the mind can shift. That healing is possible. That being human is a shared, sacred experience. And that when we struggle, it's truly an invitation to see something deeper within and to awaken more fully to who and what we truly are.

"This book is a joy to read: lighthearted, profound, and full of love—just like Mike."

~ **Aila Coats,** M.A., Coach, author of *Coaching Teens Well: A way of being with teens and their parents*

"I couldn't help but get lost in *Feeling the Flow*; it was seriously tough to set it down. Mike has this incredible way of keeping you engaged through every chapter, sharing his journey around the challenges he faced growing up and the hidden traumas he dealt with to eventually finding a way to heal from some pretty intense mental anxieties linked to his shy bladder syndrome. Honestly, I found a sense of hope in his story—not just for other people, but for myself too. What he talks about really resonates on a universal level, and he nails it perfectly. It's such a captivating and thought-provoking read!"

~ **Rick Ruppenthal,** Leadership Coach, Speaker, Three Principles Practitioner

"Michael Hurd's story speaks to the joy he discovered in finding freedom from a lifelong fear of being judged. Whether you suffer from shy bladder or shyness in expressing yourself fully, this book will illuminate what's behind your reluctance to honor yourself and be who you truly are in the world. The tried-and-true techniques and the Three Principles understanding of how your experience of fear is created reveal a path for you to step beyond your imagined thoughts of how you are being perceived and evaluated. Imagine you could peel away those ideas that keep you strategizing and coping in your unsafe world and step into joy and the freedom to be your authentic self."

~ **Marlene Cameron,** MBA, CFA, CPC, Speaker, Coach, Three Principles Practitioner

"Change begins when someone bravely shares their story. Coach and author Michael Hurd does just that, revealing his decades-long struggle with paruresis and the practical tools that helped him through. Yet at the heart of his recovery lies a deeper truth: when we see that our thoughts create our reality, insight and healing converge—turning those tools into real freedom and lasting hope. A powerful, heartfelt book for anyone facing what feels impossible."

~ **Melissa Ford,** Business and Life Coach, author of *Living Service: The Journey of a Prosperous Coach,* co-author of *When All Boats Rise: 12 Coaches on Service as the Heart of a Thriving Practice*

Feeling the *Flow*

MICHAEL HURD

Feeling the *Flow*

Creating Freedom from
Shy Bladder Syndrome

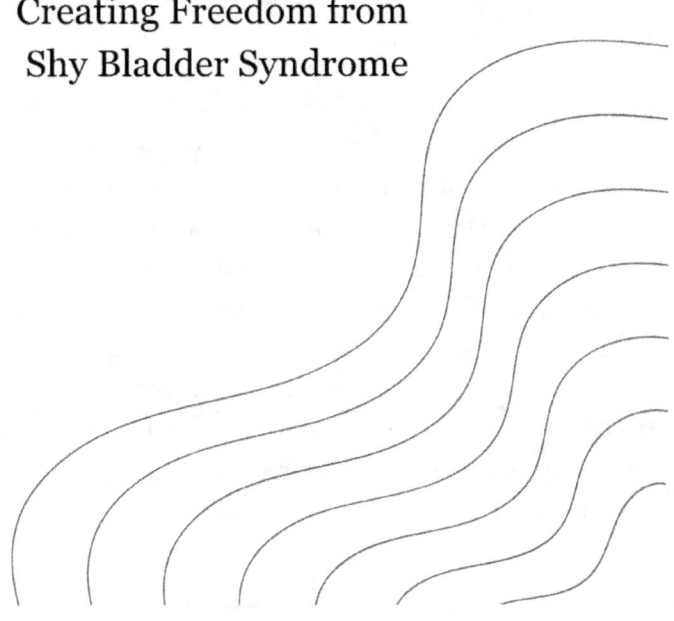

Feeling the Flow: Creating Freedom from Shy Bladder Syndrome

To Susan, Ellie and Laurel

Table of Contents

Appendices.. 113

Foreword

If you've picked up this book, you or someone you care about is likely suffering from Shy Bladder Syndrome, also known as "paruresis." This condition isn't just a little personal quirk that the word "shy" might lead you to believe. It's a recognized mental health condition and social phobia listed in the DSM-5 (*Diagnostic and Statistical Manual of Mental Disorders, fifth edition*). Statistics say nearly 7 percent of the population suffers from it.

So if you or someone you know has had this condition, then good for you for starting to read these pages!

Mike Hurd has written an invaluable addition to the shy bladder literature. If you have paruresis, you'll easily see yourself in the stories he recounts here. And if you haven't dealt with this issue yourself, your eyes will be opened to the struggle a significant number of people face in their lives.

What's it like to have a chronic shy bladder? Try being haunted by the image of "Painfully Awkward Rob Lowe" from a Direct TV ad in 2014, who says, "Fact: I can't go with other people in the room. Don't be like this me." Ouch! Or seeing yourself in the "Family Guy" character, Peter Griffin, with his internal monologue at a Fenway Park urinal: "If I don't start peeing soon, it's gonna be weird. He'll be all done and I'll still be here. Come on, Peter! Pee! Your dad fought in World War II, and you can't even pee in a urinal!

What the hell's wrong with you?"

It's not just the fact that we can't pee in proximity—or perceived proximity—to others. It's all the emotional baggage that comes with it. And of course, there's the immense physical discomfort that goes along with desperately needing to pee but being unable to do so.

As sufferers, it's not that we have "failed" at using public restrooms; it's that we've succeeded too well at avoiding them. Recovery means unlearning avoidance and re-learning how to go—not without anxiety, but alongside it.

There's a good reason why some people refer to shy bladder syndrome as "stage fright" (see, for example, Prince Harry's memoir, *Spare*). But actors still act, stage fright or not. Athletes still play. And humans still use public restrooms. For the person with paruresis, however, an intense desire and physical need to urinate cannot overcome the mind's subconscious instructions to the bladder to stay "locked up."

In this book, Mike recounts stories of being unable to go and the internal monologues that accompanied these moments. He paints a realistic and unflinching portrait of his life, recounting his anxiety, shame, fear, overplanning, and worry. These descriptions of his pre-recovery life are extremely similar to mine and to hundreds of stories I've heard from other sufferers of paruresis. And they perfectly illustrate the "ironic process" involved in this condition: no matter how hard you try not to think about this problem, the more you think about it, and the more this interferes with your ability to pee. It's a vicious cycle.

Mike also recounts his recovery—and he points to something else I've seen, namely that everyone can recover. It does take work, but as you can see from Mike's story, it is 100 percent worth the effort.

If you're a family member, significant other, or friend of someone who suffers from paruresis, this book is the best resource I've read to gain insight into what the person you care about is going through. It might not make sense to you, and it may seem illogical, and you may never have even considered what having a shy bladder is like, but after reading this book, you'll be much closer to that understanding. And even in small ways you can support someone's recovery. For example, just being patient when it takes your friend a little while longer to come out of the highway rest stop, or when they seem a little hesitant to attend that fabulous concert you've got tickets for. Your empathy will go a long way in situations like these.

As you'll read in this book, Mike has been on a journey. As Executive Director of the International Paruresis Association (IPA), I connected with him early on on his road to recovery. Mike came to the IPA in a similar manner to the 400 to 500 people who reach out to us each year. He had finally had enough of living each day wondering what the "bathroom situation" was going to be and micromanaging his daily activities related to these thoughts.

It can take amazing courage to be able to make that first step. And for the roughly ten people who do contact the IPA each week, only three or four even reply back to the resources we provide. An even smaller percentage attend our virtual workshops, virtual support groups and in-person workshops. Mike not only engaged in all these resources himself, he has gone a step further and offered himself as a resource for those who are just beginning their recovery journey.

Will your recovery be as quick? Maybe, maybe not. Each

person's experience is unique, but by steadily working at it each day, you can recover. For Mike, he reached his tipping point and then became voracious in learning more, reaching out to the IPA, attending meetings, and diligently practicing. He already had a fundamental understanding of how his recovery needed to proceed for him through his background as a business coach and his understanding of the "Three Principles" model (which you'll learn more about in this book). He jumped in with both feet and successfully leveraged three keys to shy bladder syndrome recovery:

1. Not caring what others think.
2. Having a back-up resource to turn to (you'll read about the breath-hold method and others).
3. Practicing your chosen methods until they become natural parts of your existence and you realize you don't even need to use them any longer!

Some sufferers just can't imagine what life is like on the other side of recovery. Mike is just as eloquent in sharing what his life has grown to be after his "Aha!" moment. To me, the "after" for Mike is that he feels lighter, unburdened, and amazing! He's climbed his Mount Everest. Most importantly for readers of this book, his inspiring words will help you know that you can climb yours too.

Some say the fundamentals of doing anything well in life are to "Learn, Do, and Teach." Mike has mastered these steps in sharing his journey.

I give Mike a lot of credit. Not only did he attend a live, in-person weekend workshop, but he also allowed himself to be filmed by IPA member and documentarian Steven Jackson's *Pee Shy* film crew. I don't think I would have been up for that! If you get a chance to see the film, it's a testament not only to Mike and Steven's journeys, but to the hundreds of sufferers who have been bold enough to attend a workshop with the IPA over the past thirty years. Those participants are so glad they did!

The best-selling book on paruresis recovery, *The Secret Social Phobia*, written by IPA co-founder Dr. Steven Soifer, is mentioned often by Mike in these pages. "Dr. Steve" was instrumental in my own personal recovery story. In fact, it was quite serendipitous that Mike asked me to contribute something here, as Dr. Steve and I are working on putting the finishing touches on the updated third edition of this seminal book. My key takeaway from working with Dr. Steve nearly twenty-five years ago was that no one really cares about whether I'm peeing or not or whether I have a shy bladder or not. Recognizing this fact was a major step for me.

IPA co-founder Carl Robbins says, "You can have your secret, or you can have your life!" Mike made the choice to have his life—and I'm glad he's living it to the full and sharing his story here for you.

I'm so grateful that the IPA has been here to help Mike and thousands of others—not to mention myself—since 1996. (Visit our website to learn more: paruresis.org. We're here to help!) The IPA is proud to now have Mike as a board member and on our list of Shy Bladder Center therapists and coaching professionals.

So, as you turn these pages, remember: you are not alone, and you're not broken. Whether you're just starting to face your fears or you're supporting someone you care about, know that hope and help are real. Mike's story is proof that change is possible, and that life on the other side of paruresis is not only imaginable, it's achievable. Take your time, be kind to yourself, and let this book be your guide. The journey may not always be easy, but you have a community behind you, cheering you on every step of the way.

Now, read on, and get started on your own recovery journey!

Tim Pyle, Executive Director
International Paruresis Association
Catonsville, Maryland, USA
June 2025

I: The Beginning

1.

Peeking Under the Stall

I slowly peeked under the stall with trepidation to see if any other boys were in the bathroom. I couldn't hear anything, but you can't be too careful. I knew it would help me to go pee if nobody else was around. For some reason, I just couldn't go unless I was alone in the bathroom. This was normal for me; it was all I knew. But things changed in first grade—at school I didn't have the privacy I was accustomed to at home.

Sometimes, if I was lucky, all it took was for me to be alone in a stall. So that's where I waited until I thought everybody had left the bathroom, at which point I could do my business.

Suddenly my first-grade teacher yelled at the top of her lungs, "Hurry up and finish! What's taking you so long?"

It was a sneak attack. I hadn't realized it, but she'd been holding the bathroom door open, waiting for all the boys to finish their business. I felt so embarrassed.

Well, embarrassed is not really the right word—more like *devastated* that my teacher had caught me checking to see if anyone was in the bathroom. My feelings went from a sense of relief that everyone had left the bathroom and I could finally relax to dread that I'd been caught checking.

You know that feeling when you get caught doing something embarrassing that you can't, or don't want to explain? I felt it was *my fault* that I was getting scolded. I was ashamed of myself.

I quickly left the stall, unable to pee with this new focus of attention on me. My teacher's face was crimson and purple, her veins bulging in her round neck. I wanted to run, but running was never an option.

I was used to her verbal abuse. She was a very strict teacher, someone you didn't want to cross. I would *try* not to get her upset in class. But as an energetic, curious, and stubborn first-grader, it was really hard. Which is probably why my chair was taken away when I defiantly leaned back in it too many times after she warned me not to. And then I made the unfortunate decision to sit on my desk—because I had to sit, right?

But this time, she was yelling at me in my private place: the bathroom. I didn't relieve myself until I got home that day, when I could release in my own bathroom, a relaxed and safe place.

At the time, I was innocently unaware that this bullying incident by my first-grade teacher would have such a profound impact on my brain. As a result of it—or at least, partly because of it—I struggled with a shy bladder for much of my life.

I had another bullying incident in a public bathroom around the time I was eight or nine years old, in third or fourth grade. My parents took me to a Boston Red Sox baseball game at the storied Fenway Park. What should have been a wonderful day with my parents turned into a nightmare that I've often thought of and dreamed about since then—because of the shame and embarrassment that arose from it.

I had to go to the bathroom, and my dad took me to the men's room between innings. When I walked in I saw with astonishment and shock that there were no toilets—at least not of the regular sort I recognized. Instead, there was a long ceramic wall to pee against, with drains at the bottom. I had never seen anything like this before. I'm sure I had seen urinals before, but this was not any type of urinal that I recognized. This was something altogether different. It was a free-for-all. I felt panicked, and my heart was beating fast. My dad and I stopped at the end of a long line of men waiting to approach this wall to pee. It seemed like there were hundreds of men, all lined up to release their filtered beer into what was essentially a gutter.

It was loud, it smelled, and I was mortified.

But I didn't want to disappoint my dad. So I awaited my turn, and when it arrived I stood before the wall and waited . . . and waited . . . and waited some more.

But I just couldn't go.

Behind me, impatient men grumbled at the delay. One said in a thick Boston accent, "What's taking that kid so long?"

My dad got frustrated and left me to fend for myself. I don't remember this happening, but my mother recalls being angry with him for doing so. She waited outside the restroom door to ensure I was safe. What I do remember is that I tried to access a stall, but there was a lock on it—if I recall correctly, it required coins to open.

I didn't urinate in that bathroom. It was incredibly frustrating. I *really* had to pee, but I couldn't.

I kept saying to myself, "What's wrong with me? Why can't I go like a normal person?" I judged myself for not being normal. I know that at this young age I already had chronic feelings of being "less than" or "broken." I've carried these thoughts with me for much of my life.

I've often wondered about the idea of the chicken and the egg regarding my shy bladder. That is, did I have those broken feelings because of my shy bladder, or was my shy bladder the result of something that had happened to me and how I felt about it? I eventually learned that research points to a bullying incident as the cause of some cases of the condition. If that's the case, then the feelings of being broken resulted from my thinking about the situation that I couldn't urinate in public.

I believed those thoughts for most of my life, which resulted in my insecurity about peeing in a public restroom, and the secondary worry about how it affected others, especially my parents. I was also super-worried about what my parents thought about me. I know they were frustrated. I would've done anything to make them happy with me. I know they loved me, cared about the fact that I couldn't pee in public, and wanted to help me. They were always supportive of me in other ways, such as academics and athletics. I could count on them for guidance and talk with them about pretty much anything. Except my shy bladder. This was something they didn't know how to help me with.

A Lifetime of Shy Bladder

It's interesting to me how much of my life has been spent thinking about peeing. Thinking about future "what if's":

- What if someone is in the bathroom?
- What if it's too noisy in the bathroom?
- What if it's too quiet?
- What if the urinals don't have dividers?

- What if there is a line waiting to use the bathroom?
- What if I go on a drive with my family and can't find a safe bathroom?
- What if I can't go on the airplane?
- What if we have to leave early from the concert because I can't pee there?
- What if we miss the end of the game because I need to leave early to pee?
- What if I really have to go during the meeting I'm running (or attending)? Will I have time to find a safe bathroom?

And then also thinking about the past, about a lifetime of frustration around not being able to pee in most public situations. Regret about missed opportunities. Anger over not being able to pee where "normal" people were able to.

Recently, I've realized just how much of my life I've spent thinking not just about my shy bladder, but also about the future and the past. At a certain point, with some guidance and personal understanding, I have started to notice this habit more. Interestingly, simply noticing it has brought me a degree of peace and contentment, and a calm mind, for the first time in my life. It's also helped immensely with my shy bladder.

What This Book Is About

In this book, our focus will primarily be on paruresis—the technical name for "shy bladder." I'll share what it's like dealing with the condition, and we'll explore possible causes, treatments and approaches to living with it. But because a vital part of my own journey has been understanding my thinking around my shy bladder and how it's contributed to my experience of it, we'll dive into that too. I've found that doing so has helped not just with paruresis, but in every area of my life.

So, along the way we'll also ask questions like,

- "Where in your life are you spending an inordinate amount of time thinking about the future (which hasn't happened yet) and the past (already gone)?"
- "Where are you spending time spinning over thoughts that aren't serving you?"
- "Where in your life are you (innocently) believing that your circumstances are creating your experience?"
- "When in your life have you experienced super difficult situations, and somehow made it through them?"
- "What thoughts would it serve you to pay less attention to? And also to pay more attention to?"

. . . and others, both in the context of shy bladder and elsewhere in our lives. We all innocently give energy to these kinds of thoughts and make them real. We often suffer because of it.

Ultimately this book is about my journey of recovery from a social anxiety phobia I've lived with my whole life, and I've written it to inspire your own insights and healing with shy bladder and in whatever other challenges you're facing.

I hope that before long you'll see that if I can recover, so can you.

2.

What is Paruresis?

I recently discovered that there's a scientific name for my shy bladder: *paruresis*. That's pronounced like this: "par-you-ree-sis."

Paruresis has affected my life in many ways, both positive and negative. I am the person I am today in large part because of my shy bladder, and the decisions I've made around that disability. I'll speak more about this as this book unfolds. But for now, what is paruresis?

Paruresis describes a condition in which a person has to pee, but is unable to do so. It's similar to other potentially severe anxiety disorders, such as fear of public speaking, except instead of being afraid to speak in public, people with shy bladder are afraid to pee in public.

According to the International Paruresis Association website, it is estimated that between 3-7 percent of the world's population—over 220 million people—suffers from some form of paruresis. It affects people differently: on one end of the spectrum it can be merely inconvenient and embarrassing; on the other it can be completely debilitating.

Primary Paruresis

There are two components of paruresis: *primary* and *secondary*.

Primary paruresis is the physical inability to urinate when the brain considers a situation unsafe. It is completely involuntary, involving muscles around the bladder that the brain controls unconsciously (much like how breathing, our heart beating and other functions of the autonomic nervous system typically occur without our conscious awareness or control). In brief:

> The internal urethral sphincter surrounds the beginning of the urethra, where it leaves the urinary bladder. This sphincter is smooth (involuntary) muscle. Another sphincter, the external urethral sphincter, is skeletal (voluntary) muscle and encircles the urethra where it goes through the pelvic floor. These two sphincters control the flow of urine through the urethra.[1]

When you squeeze or release your pelvic floor muscles, you contract or relax your external sphincter and can stop or start the flow of urine. Normally the involuntary internal sphincter muscle takes its lead from the external sphincter muscle and contracts or releases accordingly. In primary paruresis, however, the signaling to the involuntary internal sphincter muscle doesn't occur as expected; instead, the brain responds as though the situation is "not safe," keeping the sphincter contracted and preventing urination—no

---

[1] *Urethra*. Urethra | SEER Training. (n.d.).
https://training.seer.cancer.gov/anatomy/urinary/components/urethra.html

matter how hard you try to relax and release *or* force the flow. (You can read a more thorough explanation of how the process of urination works in *The Secret Social Phobia: Shy Bladder Syndrome (Paruresis): Second Edition.*[2])

It might seem reasonable to someone unfamiliar with paruresis to say, "Well, you should be able to go once your bladder gets full enough." But that's not how paruresis works. In my own past experience, try as I might, there have been certain situations when I have not been able to urinate, even when my bladder has seemed like it was going to burst.

Secondary Paruresis

Secondary paruresis is more about the psychological impacts of the disorder. It's about the *thought process* that happens throughout the day around everything associated with peeing.

For most people, going to pee in public is a normal biological function. Their involuntary muscles relaxes, and they are able to go. They don't have excessive thinking around peeing when they're in a restroom. In fact, in talking with people who do not have a shy bladder, I have realized that the thinking that's going on in the bathroom tends to be about anything *other* than what's actually going on in the bathroom—what happened ten minutes ago in the board meeting, what's happening later in the week, an argument with a spouse, a kid's grades, an upcoming vacation, and so on.

Having said that, since I began sharing my story, I've noticed that even if people don't have a shy bladder (most don't), they can

---

[2] Soifer, S., *Zgourides*, G. D., Himle, J., & O'Brien, N. (2020). *The Secret Social Phobia: Shy bladder syndrome (paruresis): Second Edition.* International Paruresis Association, Inc.

relate to what I'm talking about. Many have shared that they've had similar experiences or situations in their own lives that resonate with mine. Namely, there have been times when they needed to go pee but found themselves unable to do so. Maybe they were standing in front of a urinal next to someone they knew, and they suddenly felt shy. Maybe they were anxious about something else. For most people these are isolated events, and they pass quickly. Not so for people with paruresis.

The thought process for people living with paruresis, like all thought processes, varies from person to person and moment to moment. But there are some commonalities that I'll address later in the book. For now, just know that for someone living with paruresis we invest a tremendous amount of thinking and meaning around the activity of going to the bathroom.

Paruresis affects not only the person afflicted with the condition, but also the lives of their loved ones. For example, travel plans can be impacted because of concerns about bathrooms on public transportation (bus, train, plane) and at rest areas (when driving). There can be great uncertainty about being able to "go" while traveling that can impact everyone in a group.

Even casual social outings can be affected, such as going out to dinner, to a friend or family's home, to ballparks, stadiums, and school functions. Whenever there is uncertainty around going to the bathroom, it becomes an issue for the person with paruresis trying to make plans. This is because for them, every outing revolves around the thinking that goes on about whether they will able to find a "safe" bathroom. This "what if?" thinking can be paralyzing, and often results in plans being altered or even canceled.

One unfortunate thing for most people with paruresis is that we usually don't tell anyone about it. I've met many men who have never told their spouses or significant others about it. Some of these men have lived with these people for years or even decades, and have never told their loved ones or friends about their shy bladder. At first, the only person I ever told was my wife. However, up until recently I don't think she fully understood it and how my life has revolved around this challenge. My parents knew, although we never really talked about it. I never told anyone else because it was very difficult to talk about. I was afraid of what they might think—maybe that I was different, or "less than," or perhaps broken.

Fortunately, my thinking around this changed, and so did my experience of shy bladder—and I believe yours can too.

3.

Overcoming Shy Bladder

Since those childhood incidents I mentioned earlier until recently—roughly fifty-six years—my relationship with public restrooms had been pretty dismal. My life revolved around constantly seeking out accessible bathrooms.

Today, approximately one year after seeking help and embarking on my journey to overcome shy bladder, I can proudly say I've mostly recovered from this lifelong phobia. It's surreal; I often have to pinch myself to make sure I'm not dreaming.

The recovery has been twofold for me. First, I've mostly recovered from the activity of not being able to physically urinate in public.[3] This means I am able to urinate in most situations I've experimented with so far, including busy public restroom urinals with other men standing beside me. This was my Mount Everest achievement. Until recently if you'd asked me if I would ever be able to do this in my lifetime, I would have said, "No way." If you had offered to pay me a million dollars, I don't believe I could have

---

[3] Throughout the book, I will use the words urinate, pee, and void synonymously.

14

earned the prize money. In other words, it was a lifelong dream of mine to accomplish this, and that dream came true.

The second part of this condition I've recovered from is the psychological part, or secondary paruresis. As noted above, this is all the thinking around urinating that can stress us out and consequently interfere with our ability to go. In my case, I personally suffered from all of the stories I made up every time my bladder started to seem full—often before I even left the house.

- "I don't really have to go pee, but I probably should go pee now because I don't know when I'll find a safe bathroom."
- "What's going to happen when I need to go next?"
- "Where will I go?"

And once I found a bathroom it might go like this:

- "Are people wondering why it's taking me so long?"
- "Is someone going to come into the bathroom now?"
- "Can they hear me?"

In response to this kind of thinking, I would experience negative feelings caused by the thoughts I had about my condition.

- "Why can't I urinate around others?"
- "I am not a normal person."
- "I am broken."
- "I am less masculine."
- "Something is wrong with me."

Often these feelings became physical sensations: anxiety, paranoia, overwhelm and the sick feeling that started in my gut and enhanced whatever pain I was feeling in that moment.

I gave energy to all these thoughts and others. And so the thoughts were supercharged and would prevent me from relaxing enough for my brain to think it was safe enough to urinate.

My secondary paruresis is much different today than it was before, and it started to change well before my primary paruresis was corrected. I'll explain why a little later in my story.

I'm not a doctor, and I'm not providing medical advice, of course. I'm just a guy who has lived his whole life up till recently with a shy bladder. I'm also a guy who has *overcome* this condition, which has been life-changing for me.

Most importantly, if you have paruresis, I believe there is a very good chance that you, too, can also find some relief.

So in this book I'm going to continue telling my story of living with paruresis, what led me to seek help, and what I did to recover. I've learned that there isn't a one-size-fits-all approach to paruresis recovery, but I hope my story will inspire you to begin or keep going with your own process, to keep seeking answers and ideas that help with your own unique situation. Along the way I'll offer some resources to help you in your own recovery journey. Finally, I'll share a powerful insight into how our thinking impacts our lives—which helped transform mine, not only in the area of paruresis, but everywhere.

II: My Journey – Invisible Struggles

4.

My Story

I thought I was the only one on Earth who had a shy bladder.

I thought my shy bladder was all in my head. Probably because my parents used to tell me that most of my problems were "all in my head," and that I was a hypochondriac.

I've come to see that it's true: the problems were "all in my head"—though not exactly in the way they meant, which implied the solution was to just "get over it." It certainly doesn't *feel* like they're all in your head when you're in the moment. And it's not helpful knowing this unless you also know what to do about it.

Specifically, in the case of paruresis, knowing it was all in my head wasn't helpful. It was having the opposite effect because I felt that if I could just *think* better or differently, then I could fix it. That I could control my bladder if I *just tried harder*, or differently.

That's not how paruresis works. In fact, trying harder seems to have the opposite effect in that it makes it even more challenging to go. Have you ever tried to stop thinking about something? To stop being afraid of something? That's the psychological component.

As we have seen, it is believed that the physical component to it develops due to some type of psychologically impactful experience, like bullying. When the brain believes that the situation is "unsafe," it keeps the sphincter muscles that control the bladder tight and unable to relax.

I didn't know any of this until recently. As I say, I thought I was the only one in the world with this problem. This wasn't because I'm against seeking help for things. I've sought help for other issues I've faced, such as Lyme disease, shoulder pain and toxic mold exposure. And I've seen therapists for issues I was having difficulty figuring out on my own.

But my shy bladder . . . nope. I didn't think there was a cure for it. I couldn't even fathom that there were other people in the world who had the same problem. I felt so strongly about this that I never even did an Internet search for it.

If I had, I might have found the International Paruresis Association (IPA) many years ago. It was founded in 1996, right around the birth of the Internet as we know it. But I never knew it existed until the end of 2023.

I didn't seek help for my paruresis until I decided that I both wanted help and was open to getting it. This moment came after an extremely uncomfortable flight in November of 2023, when I was unable to use the airplane bathroom. I'll share that story later.

~

I have found that everyone living with paruresis has different comfort levels or baselines for what their brain considers safe and unsafe—which correlates to voiding or not voiding in a urination attempt.

To get a sense of what my safe or unsafe situations were prior to my recovery, here are some different bathroom settings I considered easy and not easy in terms of urinating. If you suffer or have suffered from paruresis, I suspect you could make your own list.

Situations I considered easy or relatively easy:

- My own bathroom.
- My own bathroom with other people in the house.
- A bathroom when my wife is in the same bathroom.
- A friend's or family member's home.
- Many private bathrooms, like a Starbucks or hotel bathroom, if it was a single-person bathroom with a lock on the door and no one was waiting for me.
- I'm a competitive swimmer, and sometimes I could go before practice in a busy bathroom. Sometimes not. But I could always go after I'd been swimming a hard workout and my body was physically exhausted.

Here's where it would get uneasy for me:

- If I thought someone was waiting for me, I usually could not go. Like on an airplane or in a restaurant, gas station, or supermarket with a small restroom.
- If someone jiggled the lock on the bathroom door. (Side note: I would love to send the person who invented the lock that turns red or green depending on the occupancy a thank-you card.)
- A large public bathroom, like in a mall, restaurant, or airport. Sometimes I could go sitting down in a private stall, but

other times I couldn't. A lot of this had to do with my thinking around the design of the stall. If it had wide gaps between the walls, floor and ceiling, or if there were only one or two stalls, then it was harder for me. I would feel like someone was watching or waiting for me, or that they could hear me.

Situations which were too hard, where I wouldn't even try:

- A public bathroom with a wall lined with urinals. Think ballparks, concert stadiums, large restaurants, busy bars, busy hotels, airports, highway rest areas, train stations, bus stations, convention centers, department stores, malls, amusement parks. No-go.

~

As I've said, living with paruresis has been an underlying reason for many of the decisions I've made in my life. I'm not saying I would necessarily change anything, or that my life has turned out bad in any way. Just the contrary, actually. I have a wonderful life with my wife of thirty-three years, two beautiful, amazing daughters, and two wonderful sons-in-law. A great home and a career I enjoy. Life is great. My paruresis has helped make me the person I am today: a loving, compassionate father and friend, and I think an overall good, conscientious, hard-working person.

But I've definitely suffered from this condition and I'm glad I started the work to overcome it.

5.

The YMCA

Looking back on my journey, I see how much living with a shy bladder shaped my reality. From the scary, smelly stalls of my first-grade bathroom to the daunting rows of urinals at Fenway park, each experience left a mark of both fear and resilience.

I always seemed to figure out ways to cope with my shy bladder in and around locker rooms. I don't have too many negative memories of incidents from this time in my life, which included my teenage years, probably because I got creative about how I could find a friendly bathroom. Coping with paruresis just became a normal part of my life.

There were even brief moments of comfort during my teen years. I found unexpected sanctuaries in places like the YMCA. In its busy hallways, surrounded by camaraderie and activity, I could escape the chaos of adolescence, if only for a little while. Being on both the YMCA 18-and-under swim team and the high school swim team, I spent a lot of time at our YMCA after school. It was an easy walk to the Y from both junior high and high school. We lived several miles away from town, so I would walk from school to the

Y to swim, and I would study at the nearby library before and between double workouts.

That said, the YMCA's locker room bathroom was not a safe place for me. It was smelly and old, and the single toilet was in a "room" that had no doors; it was more like an open walk-through closet between the locker room and the showers leading to the pool. Everyone needed to pass by it. There was absolutely no privacy. To add to the difficulty, the pre-teen and early teen boys' locker-room was absolute chaos. Changing before and after swim practice involved a lot of spitting, towel snapping, "titty twisters," yelling, and hyper-energy that was only marginally controlled by the exhausting workouts.

The only time I was able to use that bathroom was in between swim sets, when my body was so tired that it allowed the internal sphincter muscle to relax enough to go. I've been fortunate that this has been the case throughout my life—when I'm physically exhausted from a hard workout or swim race, it's easy for me to go to the bathroom. Outside of this situation, however, the Y was a hard place for me to find a bathroom I could use. I often hear swimmers say that swimming is their "happy place." That it is a place that helps them relax and forget their troubles. Swimming has also been my happy place, but for the primary reason of being a place where I can easily pee at a urinal with relative ease.

At some point in my middle teens, my father reserved a locker in the men's locker room, which had more private toilets. It was also empty during our mid- to late-afternoon swim team workouts. I talked him into letting me use his locker, mostly for the privacy it provided me. I considered this area my oasis. I also remember getting a little pushback about using the men's locker room from some adult members, but my dad defended me, and I was super grateful for it.

6.

The Hockey Game

When I think back to my childhood, I remember warmth and adventure. From the love of my family, to exploring our acres of wooded property in the countryside, to the excitement of our trips and vacations, those early years were filled with happiness. Through it all, my shy bladder was always there, a quirky part of me that I learned to live with instead of fight against. It was just another piece of the puzzle, something I accepted and worked around as I enjoyed life to the fullest.

One of my favorite memories is of going to hockey games with my Aunt Brenda when I was a teenager. We were fans of a minor league hockey team called the Maine Mariners. They played their games at the Portland Civic Center in Portland, Maine, which was about a forty-minute drive from where we lived. I loved watching the Maine Mariners: the excitement of the crowd, the fast pace of the hockey games, the Zamboni clearing the ice between periods, the fights (minor league hockey in the 1980s), and more. We went to many playoff games.

All that said, I dreaded using the bathrooms at hockey games. There was one time I *really* had to use the bathroom, but I knew it would be challenging in that environment. There were only a few stalls, with wide gaps between the stall walls, and from what I can remember the urinals did not have dividers between them (to be honest, even if they'd had dividers, I don't think I could have used them).

So, one trick I tried was to wash my hands first, while I waited for the bathroom to empty. After a few minutes of thorough handwashing, the bathroom emptied enough for me to give it a go, and I went into a stall to try.

Stalls in men's rooms are often disgusting; men tend to urinate all over the seat, especially at concerts or sporting events. I'm not sure why, other than maybe the alcohol-addled brain prevents them from being able to lift the seat. So sitting down in this stall was not an option. This was well before the era of paper seat covers; besides which, even if they'd had covers back then the urine on the toilet seat would've soaked right through. So, I stayed standing, zipped down and gave it a try.

Suddenly I heard another teen nearby say to his friend, "Did you see that? That guy washed his hands *before* he went to the bathroom. What a retard."

I couldn't believe he was talking about me. I wanted to hide, but there was nowhere to run to. Needless to say, I was not able to pee. This was not a safe place to urinate, and my brain shut down my sphincter muscles. I zipped up and left the bathroom without looking at them.

I stayed uncomfortable for the rest of the game. And although I don't remember it, I'm sure I made an excuse to stop at a McDonald's to pee on the way home.

7.

Bar Hopping

College was where I first encountered alcohol, and in some ways, it became a peculiar ally in my battle with paruresis. Not necessarily because it miraculously solved my bladder woes—that was still a subconscious battle—but because it dulled the edge of my worries about finding a suitable restroom. It was as if alcohol cast a blanket over my anxieties, allowing me to care less about the surroundings or the lengths I went to in search of a friendly restroom. Yet, in hindsight, it also led me down perilous paths, blurring my judgment and prompting risky, alcohol-fueled decisions.

I remember being at a bar with some friends in the Boston area. We were out for a good time. I started drinking, was having a great time, and soon had to use the bathroom. Having to go to the bathroom usually turned my *great* time into one of high anxiety, and this situation was no different. Although I tried going to the bar restroom, it was way too busy, and my bladder muscle just wouldn't relax.

Although this was over thirty-five years ago, I remember as clearly as if I were still there how frustrating it was. Thinking back brings a flood of feelings and takes me completely out of the present

28

moment. (As a side note, it's interesting how we "live" in the experience of our thinking, and it can pull us away from our present "reality," so that our reality becomes whatever we are thinking about.)

What I did next is what I would often do when I went out to bars drinking. I left the bar to find a place that I could go pee. It seemed logical to me. My alcohol-infused brain thought this was a great idea, although I realize now that it was a very bad one. My friends were drinking and trying to pick up college girls, and they had no idea I was leaving.

In this particular case, I quickly found a restaurant nearby and was able to void. But in many situations, even when leaving the bar was not a safe idea because of the part of town it was in, this rarely stopped me. Partly because I really had to go, and partly because alcohol clouded my judgement. I would find an alley or walk around an unfamiliar city by myself, often drunk, to find someplace where I could go. It's ironic that in my quest for a "safe" toilet I was risking getting mugged or worse. Thinking back to the many times I've done this in my life, I'm probably lucky to be alive today.

8.

To Grandmother's House We Go

In my experience, using the bathroom at someone else's house has usually been manageable. I recognize how fortunate I am, as many individuals struggling with paruresis don't have the same experience. However, it hasn't always been smooth sailing for me. There was a time when even my grandparents' home posed a challenge, where the familiar surroundings didn't offer the comfort I needed to ease my nerves.

Growing up, I had many Thanksgiving dinners at my grandparents'. They had one bathroom in their small home, and I had a lot of thoughts about using it.

- "What if someone else is waiting to use the bathroom?"
- "What if someone opens the door while I'm trying to go?"
- "Is it taking me too long to try and go right now?"

These questions were usually reserved for more public places, but for some reason they would come up for me when I was visiting my grandparents. Probably because their bathroom had a sliding wooden door that didn't soundproof anything. It wiggled a little, too, and if people came in and out of the front door of the house, the bathroom door would rattle and disturb me. Also, when I was in there I could hear everyone in the kitchen talking, so I was sure they could hear me peeing (or not peeing). In short, I believed the whole world could hear what was or wasn't happening.

Thanksgiving was a particularly difficult time because about twenty people gathered at the house. It's an interesting blend of good and bad memories for me: getting together as a family, eating delicious food and watching the Thanksgiving football games . . . and all of this almost completely overshadowed by anxiety about using the bathroom with a house full of people.

Although none of these thoughts were really true, they were true for me at that moment. I know now that nobody cared what I was doing, and certainly nobody was timing me, but this didn't make my thinking about it any more or less real to me at the time. The fact that I often thought I was taking too long probably kept me in the bathroom even longer. It's amazing the stories we tell ourselves and believe.

9.

The Office

As I moved from the formative years of adolescence into the complexities of adulthood and corporate life, my journey often led me into the bustling corridors of office buildings. Here, the challenges of navigating bathrooms took on a whole new dimension.

Early in my career I worked at a car dealership. Fortunately we had a bathroom with a lock on the door. It was just outside my office, so I could see if it was busy or not, and could lock the door behind me when I went in. If someone tried to enter while I was in there, however, that would make the urine crawl back up into my bladder (or so it seemed). It was a frustrating and uncomfortable feeling where I would often get so close to starting the process to void that I could feel the urine about to exit my body, but the sound of someone jiggling the lock would trigger my brain to say "UNSAFE SITUATION." And the best I could hope for at that point was a meager dribble.

Later in my work life, I became a financial consultant in a large office building in Portland, Maine. We had one bathroom for around twenty men, and it was rare to find it empty. Fortunately for me, I've usually been able to go while sitting down in a stall. If I stayed in there long enough, the bathroom would empty and I'd be able to go. Not always, but usually. Somehow, I was able to cope and make it work but, gosh, did I have a lot of thinking about it. I also crafted a number of coping strategies, like finding other bathrooms in the building or in nearby businesses, restaurants and hotels.

Soon after this, I became a "road warrior" and spent most of my time either working from home or traveling. The working from home was great, but traveling generated much thinking around finding a bathroom. In addition, something about being able to go anytime I wanted to when at home was counterproductive to being able to go while I was traveling. For one thing, I've learned that the bladder is designed to void when there is a strong urge to go. That urge feels different to me when I'm home. I've realized that I often go to the bathroom when my bladder really isn't full. In other words, I haven't trained my bladder very well. So I'd be driving or traveling through airports and think I had to void, but I really didn't have to go badly enough . . . especially in public. Another reason working from home was counterproductive for me is that I had much less "practice" going in public. With long periods of time at home, it was less likely I'd have a situation to try a public bathroom, and a much bigger deal when I traveled.

The stall strategy I mentioned earlier was always my "go-to" in a busy bathroom. But I also started realizing that certain hotels or gas stations had "safe" bathrooms to use. Not always, but usually. This reassured me that I could typically travel without panicking about finding a bathroom. Although never certain of the "how," I always had a reasonable hope that it would work out.

At one point in my career, I worked for a large, publicly traded company. I was on the road most of the time, but occasionally we visited corporate headquarters for meetings.

I would load up with coffee to get me through the day, but this was of course a double-edged, caffeinated sword, and it quickly led to my having to use the bathroom. In this case, there was no leaving the building to find a "safe" spot to go. The men's bathrooms here had two urinals and two stalls each. The floor on which my meetings were held was busy, and this meant there was almost always someone in the bathroom.

Queue the busy thinking around this situation! The thought bunnies started hopping around in my head, propagating wildly (as bunnies do).

We all took breaks at the same time, so it was usually very difficult for me to relax enough to urinate at a urinal. I couldn't go into the bathroom without my co-workers. If I could, I sat down in a stall, and this sometimes worked.

Other times, I took a bathroom break in between the scheduled breaks. This created a lot of thoughts like, "They must be wondering why I'm taking a break now. We just had one!" It's never comfortable leaving during a meeting; for someone with paruresis it can be even more uncomfortable.

Another tactic I employed was "exploring" other floors—pretending to check out how other departments operated—while looking for bathrooms that weren't as busy. This sometimes worked, and it became one of my go-to strategies in a corporate setting.

As you might imagine, situations like these can be quite stressful to someone with a shy bladder. The "what if's" about the bathroom build on each other until they often become overwhelming. Add to that whatever is going on at work, and it can make for a nasty cocktail of busy thinking and physical discomfort.

10.

How Much Can One Person Think About Bathrooms?

I often joke with my wife that I can tell her about all the shy bladder-friendly restrooms anywhere in New England. This isn't completely true, but it's close enough. The knowledge I've gained is the result of years of struggle.

For many years I traveled by car around New England (Maine, Massachusetts, New Hampshire, Vermont, Rhode Island, and Connecticut) for business. One year I logged over 50,000 miles driving around the region. For someone with a shy bladder, this sort of travel can be brutal, and it often was for me. The amount of brain space taken up with negative bathroom-related thinking was overwhelming.

In my "research" I found that a bathroom would either be "friendly" or "not friendly" to my shy bladder. Friendly meant I could always or usually go there. A friendly bathroom was one where it was easy for me to urinate, and where my brain believed it was safe to do so. For example, it might be a single-occupancy bathroom.

However, a single-use bathroom didn't always mean it was a safe bathroom for me. For example, if it was the only bathroom in the establishment and there were people waiting—or even the potential for people waiting—while I tried to go, it might not work. I believed all my thinking around what it meant if people were waiting for me: they would get impatient, they'd tap their feet, they'd think something was wrong with me . . . This was all in my head, but it still felt real to me.

Given this, if there was more than one single-occupancy bathroom in the same establishment, my odds of going were much higher.

A friendly bathroom could also be a multiple-occupancy bathroom with some sort of privacy built in. For example, where the stalls are like closets— the walls are flush with the floor and the solid door closes and locks. Essentially, it's like being in a closet.

An unfriendly bathroom was one that had little to no privacy. The urinals had no dividers. The stalls had wide gaps between the floor and ceiling. Those gaps have always made me think that a six-year-old was hired to design and install them—someone who didn't care about or understand a certain level of privacy. Or maybe that the project was outsourced to the lowest bidder—who shaved a few dollars off the bid by skimping on wall costs. Who says they have to touch the floor or ceiling? It's almost like the builders were told to "Design this bathroom stall in a manner that provides the occupant no privacy—and then make it *worse* than you think THAT should be." I have no engineering experience, yet I am confident I could build a better stall than many I have seen in my travels.

Here's a rundown of some the better-known places I've experienced to stop for a restroom break:

- Gas station bathrooms: some are friendly, some aren't. Some have a single use; some have more open use. Single use is great, if nobody jiggles the door handle.
- Coffee Shops: usually friendly, as most have single-use bathrooms. But if someone jiggles the door handle, forget it.
- Hotels: Often a great option. Most have private or semi-private bathrooms. And certain hours of the day (not check-in or check-out times) are generally not busy. I have figured out which hotels are friendly and which are not.
- Public Rest Areas: Usually terrible options, completely unfriendly. Most are government-funded, with lines of urinals without dividers (the short wall between urinals). Also, the locks are often broken in the stalls. And if they have stalls, the walls are so low, or the corner gaps are so wide, you might as well be out in the open. At least that is what someone living with paruresis thinks.
- Fast-food Restaurants: It depends. Some are good, some are okay, and some are terrible. It really depends on the chain of restaurants, and even the local ownership. You can tell when a fast-food restaurant is cutting corners in their design of the bathroom.

You can imagine the amount of thought it takes to keep track of all of this. Or maybe you can't. Most people don't even think about it. Must go to the bathroom? Great, let's find the closest restroom. In and out. Done.

I remember on one business trip my boss was riding along with me. I was not about to tell him I couldn't use a public restroom. No way. We stopped at a rest area, and I wasn't able to go. Try as I might, even sitting down in a stall, I could not go. Fortunately, I have a "steel bladder" and was able to hold it long enough to make it to our next appointment, where there was a bathroom that was friendly.

How much brain bandwidth have I spent around finding a friendly bathroom? How much chatter has run through my head, generating anxiety and storytelling around going to the bathroom? This chapter gives you just a hint of that.

The funny thing is, my concern about being able to go and the stories I was telling myself were a huge part of why I couldn't go in the first place. They were, in effect, a self-fulfilling prophecy. I had put myself at the mercy of my thinking.

11.

My Tipping Point

In November of 2023 I was on a five-and-a-half-hour flight from Las Vegas to Baltimore, coming home from a business convention. I was a little worried when I boarded the plane because I hadn't done the "dehydration trick" that I normally do.

It wasn't really much of a trick—I would just drink absolutely nothing before the long flight in the hope that I therefore wouldn't have to go to the bathroom. It usually worked, but there are bad side effects of doing the dehydration trick, including headaches and tiredness. Obviously, it's not a healthy practice, but sometimes it seemed the best thing to do.

Unfortunately I hadn't done it this time. And to make matters worse, I had tried to time it so I could use one of those premium business-lounge bathrooms at the airport, where I was usually assured a friendly space.

This time, as I approached the desk to check in, I knew that the experience was going to be stressful (at least that's the story I made up at the time). The man in front of me was arguing with the lounge employee regarding his status and whether he was allowed to enter the facility. As the argument unfolded, I kept looking at my watch. I needed to board my plane soon.

Finally, the agent gave in and let the man into the lounge. I quickly checked in and made a beeline to the bathroom. Unfortunately, one of the stalls was out of order and the other was occupied. Even worse, another person was in front of me waiting to use the stall.

You have to be kidding me! I thought, feeling more than a hint of panic. There was a urinal, but that was out of the question.

I made the decision to board my plane without using the bathroom ahead of time.

A couple hours into my flight, the need to urinate became urgent. I was on an older Boeing 737, one of the absolute worst configurations on a cross-continent trip for someone who has a shy bladder. It must have been designed and approved by trolls. The plane has a first-class section with its own lavatory, and another two restrooms in the back for coach passengers (which included me on this flight). This meant that 112 of the 124 total passengers were forced to use the two rear lavatories, while the twelve people in first class and the flight crew could use the front bathroom. The result? A line of people eight to ten deep for the entire flight waiting to use the rear lavatory. Someone with a shy bladder notices these things.

I decided to try using the lavatory, waiting in the long line. However, when I eventually got in there, I couldn't go. Tricks or coping mechanisms rarely worked (not that I had many at my disposal), and they didn't this time either. Sometimes I could listen to music on my phone with noise cancelling headphones; I think this would trick my brain into listening to the music rather than the negative pee chatter going on in my head. But this "solution" delivered inconsistent results, and this was one of those days where it didn't work. If I felt like people were waiting, my brain would say "no-go," and my bladder muscle would tighten up. Up to this point, there was nothing I had been able to find to make that muscle relax. So, disappointed, I walked back to my seat.

My bladder almost burst on this trip back from Las Vegas. Technically that's not true—I've recently learned that bladders can't *actually* burst. But it sure felt like it was going to happen. I suffered on that flight.

The best thing about this moment was that it became my tipping point. Because of it, I finally surrendered and asked the universe, and my wife, for help.

III. Recovery

12.

One Year Later

It hardly seems like I'm the same person today that I was a year ago. As I write this, it's been exactly one year since the trip that changed my life. I just got home from the same business convention I'd attended the previous year, and my experience was completely different this time around. It's truly amazing the progress I've made.

For one thing, I didn't have *any* thinking about the future! Let me explain. For my whole life I've been preoccupied with what I thought could happen regarding my shy bladder and my ability to go. For a business trip, this would start many days before my trip. I would have an enormous amount of thinking about all of the made-up situations where it would be difficult to use the bathroom. And most of those situations would come true—although eventually I would find a bathroom to use.

Now that weight of negative thought was gone, replaced with calm thinking or no thinking at all about my future bathroom situations. I knew I could find a place to void—and then actually urinate—when I needed to.

There were other major differences with this trip compared to my pre-recovery travel days. For starters, my trip to the airport was different. I had no thinking before I left the house about how and when I should use the bathroom before arriving at the airport. I had a large glass of water to stay hydrated. Normally, I would have stopped at the Hilton Garden Inn next to the airport so I could use their bathroom; it's not a busy one and has always been my go-to before flights. This trip I went straight to the airport. Another trick I used to do was to use the bathroom in the general airport waiting area. It's a quiet bathroom that my brain had always considered safe, as long as nobody else was in it.

This trip I skipped that bathroom. I didn't really have to go yet, and I figured I'd try going in one of the bathrooms on the other side of security—which I ended up doing.

After my breakfast, I had about thirty minutes to boarding. Portland, Maine has a relatively new terminal, but it has always seemed to me that they have a very small bathroom for the size of the airport. They actually have two bathrooms on the departure side of security. Both are small, and in the past I would never try to use them unless I could sit down in a stall. Even then, because there was usually a line waiting, this would be difficult or impossible for me because of my anxiety over my thinking about taking too long in the stall.

That day was different, though. I walked by the men's room and saw a line stretching out the entrance. This is a situation I would definitely have passed on before, and instead tried my luck at the restroom wherever my layover was. This time, however, I waited in line. I was going to try out my new breath-holding technique (which I share a little later in this book). I patiently waited for my turn, walked up to the urinal and started to hold my breath.

I waited. The man next to me left and was replaced by a new person. The same thing happened in the urinal to his left. There were only three urinals, and I seemed to be at mine for much longer than my urinal neighbors. But I didn't care. I ignored the negative chatter in my head, such as, "Hey, it's taking you wayyy longer than everyone else. The guys behind you must be glaring at you right now!"

I kept telling myself that there are many reasons why it may take a person longer than others, and nobody *really* cares. I kept holding my breath to the point where my gasp reflex started kicking in . . . then I kept holding it past that point and started to pee! What an incredible experience! I was able to void with a long line behind me. I'd never been able to do this before. How incredible.

Flying to Vegas brought me through Nashville as a connector. As there were no lounges I could use there, the old me would have worried the whole flight about finding a safe bathroom. Instead, I enjoyed my flight, and even had a cup of coffee while in the air. I was able to use the airplane bathroom just fine—a new, fun experience for me.

I arrived in Las Vegas excited about the convention I was about to attend. I had newfound confidence that I could use the bathroom in any setting, and was excited to see what unfolded during the week.

The morning the convention started I went to Starbucks for breakfast. A year ago, I would never have done this. My old strategy was to dehydrate myself so I wouldn't have to use the bathroom too often. This year, I started my day at Starbucks and had not one, but two Grande dark roasts, to complement my oatmeal breakfast. In addition, I bought a large water to drink at the event.

Soon after I arrived at the Venetian hotel, I went into the casino bathroom on the way to the convention center. With a full bladder, I was able to pee alongside other men at a urinal. My convention was off to a great start!

I won't list the details of every bathroom experience, but I do want to mention that I spent very little time thinking about bathrooms during the convention. One memorable moment was when I went into a bathroom in the downstairs area of the convention center. The previous year this had been scary as hell for me, and I was only able to use the corner stall. This year I repeatedly used the urinals, which had small dividers, and I used them while the restroom was busy. This was a huge accomplishment for me. Not only was I able to void my bladder, but I had very little thinking about it. I just went in, did my business, washed my hands and left. Actually, the washing my hands part was the hardest because I can never figure out those automatic sensors.

Another remarkable bathroom situation I remember from this trip, took place during one of my convention breaks. In the past, I would use the time during the break to trek to my hotel room, which was a completely safe place for me (unless I timed it during housekeeping, which was an occasional risk). This time, however, I went to the public restroom outside the convention area. And one of the other attendees went in at the same time. Historically in that situation I would either use a stall and sit down to try to go, or I would pretend to use the urinal and then head up to my hotel room to go.

This time was different. I was not only able to start my flow alongside the other person, but we were actually having a conversation at the same time! This may not seem like a big deal to you, but to me it was *huge*. It was just like it happens on television or the movies. It was so weird, but cool. I kept thinking to myself, "Relax, you're just having a conversation while peeing"—but also, "How amazingly cool is this?" Meanwhile, the other person had no idea how much of a milestone this was for me and what was really going through my head. Do we ever know what is going through someone else's head?

This trip demonstrated that I could go in nearly every situation. At the convention center, at the casino, and at many restaurants around Las Vegas, I marked my territory. The couple of times I couldn't go, it wasn't a big deal to me; I just tried again a little later and was able to go. I have found that this situation is true for many people who *don't* generally have a shy bladder. Sometimes you just can't go! The major difference for me from the previous year was that I didn't make any meaning about it.

Urinating while standing at the urinal was my Mount Everest. The highest achievement I could have hoped for in my shy bladder journey. I never thought I'd be able to do it. I'd always had hope, but in truth I never thought it would happen. Yet here I was: I had completely overcome my decades-old fear of peeing in public.

How did I get to this point where I could pee pretty much anytime, anywhere? It all started with the previous year's traumatic flight home from Vegas.

13.

My Recovery

Shortly after that five-and-a-half-hour return trip from Vegas—where I couldn't use the restroom the entire time, despite desperately needing to—I started finding some resources to help me.

The International Paruresis Association

It began with my wife, who did an internet search and found an organization that was created to help people just like me: The International Paruresis Association (IPA). The IPA (https://www.paruresis.org) was created to help people with shy bladders recover from the condition. I could not believe there was a whole website dedicated to helping people suffering from a shy bladder! How amazing!

I dove in and read the website from front to back. I started watching videos and reading the articles and books they recommended. I had never heard the term "shy bladder syndrome" before, and definitely not the scientific name of "paruresis." *How do I even pronounce this?* was the first thought I had!

As I surfed through the different tabs, articles and videos, a whole new world started to unfold in front of my eyes. It's funny how one second we can be living in despair, and another second we are filled with love and hope—the only difference being the thought we are believing.

The experience of finding this organization was surreal to me. I'd spent my whole life up to that point thinking that I was the only person who had a shy bladder, and now I had discovered a whole world of people who were suffering just like me. I got goosebumps. New worlds of possibility now existed, where before there was just a hope of "getting through" or coping. I started to get excited about potentially healing.

I reached out to the IPA executive director, Tim Pyle, and scheduled a one-on-one Zoom meeting with him. Tim was one of the first people in my life, other than my wife, with whom I shared my experiences with shy bladder. He's an amazing, compassionate person who—I learned—had suffered with the same condition as me. It was a very emotional and wonderful experience. I got to hear Tim's story about living with paruresis, and I also shared mine. This was the first time I had talked with someone else who suffered from paruresis. As the conversation unfolded, a rainbow of emotions unfolded with it. I was surprised, amazed, and happy that I found the IPA and all of the new resources to help me. Tim has a personality that put me at ease very quickly. He is very empathetic and a terrific listener. I felt as if I had made a new friend very quickly.

I was also a bit sad and frustrated that it had taken me this long to find these amazing resources. But these regretful feelings didn't last long.

The Secret Social Phobia

After that conversation I jumped right in, and read an amazing book called *The Secret Social Phobia: Shy Bladder Syndrome (Paruresis)* by S. Soifer, G. Zgourides, J. Himle, & N. O'Brien (IPA, Inc. 2020). This is the definitive book on shy bladder. It described in detail what I've been living with for fifty years, along with offering potential explanations as to how it might have started and giving practical techniques and tips on how to start my recovery process. It also shared many stories of people just like me who have suffered from paruresis. The book references many scientific resources and both anecdotal and evidence-based research as well. If you are suffering from paruresis and can only use one resource to help in your recovery, this is the one to get.

Support Groups and Workshops

Then I attended my first virtual support group. From the start of the meeting I was blown away with the positive feelings. I heard many other people's stories, which reaffirmed that I was not alone with this condition. It was very emotional to learn that other people had the same condition as me. Our stories were different, and our experiences were as well. But everyone was suffering because of the shared condition of shy bladder syndrome. I also shared my own story, finally talking about something I had bottled up inside for decades. It was like pressing the pressure release on a coffee pot, finally being able to tell my story to others in an environment where I knew there was no judgement. The process of listening to other people's stories and telling my own was very liberating and healing. I had never attended a support group before, and I suddenly saw why they are so popular and effective.

Next, I signed up for a virtual workshop. Here I learned a lot about the biology of the bladder and what causes paruresis, as well as some techniques that help people recover. These include graduated exposure, cognitive behavioral therapy (CBT), and breath holding. I'll share a little bit about some of these below, and you can also refer to the Resources section at the end of the book to find ways to learn more about them. (I've also included a chapter later in the book specifically about my experiences with the breath-holding technique.) According to the IPA website, "Many studies show that cognitive-behavioral therapy over 8-12 sessions or a weekend workshop helps at least 4 out of 5 sufferers."[4]

Graduated Exposure

During the workshop we quickly jumped right into practicing the graduated exposure technique. Graduated exposure is a process whereby you retrain the brain to learn what a "safe" or "scary" environment is by gradually exposing yourself to more and more fearful situations. In the virtual workshop environment, we all drank a ton of fluid (called fluid-loading) and then paired up with a pee buddy and started practicing. For me, a safe situation was being in my home bathroom while leaving my phone with the Zoom meeting on it in the living room; I knew my "pee buddy" was there and waiting for me, but he couldn't hear me at first. I gradually exposed myself to scarier situations, with the scariest being having my pee buddy virtually stand beside me, via zoom (with the phone camera pointed at my head on the bathroom countertop) while I

---

[4] https://paruresis.org/shy-bladder-facts/

voided. This simulated a real life men's room situation, as best we could. Graduated exposure helped me take baby steps towards my end goal of wanting to be able to urinate at a public urinal with other men standing nearby. I practiced peeing with a pee buddy starting at a point where I was comfortable, then gradually getting more and more uncomfortable as the practice went on.

Breath Holding

Breath holding is different. It was ultimately a complete gamechanger for me, and I dedicate a more detailed chapter to my experiences with it—and how to learn more about it—later in this book. With this technique you essentially hold your breath until the bladder muscle relaxes. It's uncomfortable, but for me it's highly effective. When I was first learning this technique, I was unsuccessful. Then I realized I wasn't holding my breath long enough. So I made the decision to hold my breath until it worked—which, I found, was shortly after my reflexes started making me want to gasp for breath. My stomach would lurch as my lungs begged me to breathe, and if I held it just past that point, my sphincter muscle relaxed and I was able to urinate.

Incredibly, as I continued to practice the breath-holding technique, I found I could urinate in situations that had previously seemed impossible. (A reminder to please talk with your physician before trying this or any other techniques described in this book, not least if you have any health issues, such as a heart condition).

A New Relationship with My Thinking

What has happened since learning these techniques, and gaining a better understanding of how our minds work, is nothing short of miraculous.

After attending the virtual workshop, my confidence increased, and I started practicing at a local Walmart, first using graduated exposure and then breath holding (after watching a video on it). I didn't urinate every time, but I found I was okay with that. It's also true that this particular bathroom was not the most challenging, as it was hit or miss whether or not it would be busy. This meant there was a good chance I could use this bathroom. So it was good practice, and it helped me gain greater confidence, but it wasn't a true test; that, I knew, was coming up, because I was scheduled to attend another convention in Vegas soon.

I was starting to appreciate the role that my thinking had regarding my experience living with shy bladder syndrome. I recognized that I had been placing a tremendous amount of meaning on the success or failure of being able to pee. One thing I learned at the virtual workshop was that the IPA community didn't even use the word "failure" when describing "not peeing." They used the word "misfire."

I liked that. It wasn't a failure when I couldn't go. *I* wasn't a failure for not being able to go. It was just a misfire. I started to observe it neutrally when I didn't go every time, and I didn't create any meaning about it. I simply couldn't go at that time. I'd had a misfire. I realized for the first time in my life that my peeing or not peeing could not affect how I felt about myself. It was my *thoughts* that affected my experience of being able to pee or not at any given time, and how I felt about myself.

It was how I *thought* about it. This new understanding, combined with the techniques I was now practicing regularly, changed everything.

14.

What Happens in Vegas

Then I went back to Las Vegas, where I could practice big time!

The day I was scheduled to travel, I woke up and had a glass of water. This may not seem like a big deal, but it wasn't normal for me to drink anything on a long travel day. At the airport I drank a coffee. Again, not normal. But my layover was at Baltimore Washington International Airport (BWI) and I was eager to try their new restroom design.

I'm glad I did. Wow . . . the restrooms are amazing at BWI. Following their renovations, the urinals are separated by solid, substantial dividers for increased privacy. And the stalls have walls flush with the floor and a solid door that closes. Basically, you're in your own private space. Amazing.

The positive experience of being able to confidently urinate in the BWI restroom and my recent practicing at Walmart gave me the confidence to drink liquids at the airport—in preparation for making an attempt to urinate in the lavatory on the plane. So I drank up and boarded . . . and told myself that I would use the lav when I had to go. I planned on trying the breathholding technique. Furthermore, I decided I would either *go* or *pass out*. One way or the other, something big was going to transpire in that lavatory.

I boarded the plane; we took off and I was excited for the trip. Also of note, I flew Southwest Airlines, which does not have a first-class section. Consequently, the wait for the bathroom was much shorter than it had been when I'd flown in November and been unable to go. It seemed amazing how much opening the front lavatory to the entire plane reduced bathroom wait times.

When the flight crew served us the first time, I ordered a coffee *and* a water. Unprecedented. I was really going to do this!

About two hours into the flight, the moment of truth arrived. I really had to go. So I went back to the lavatory, entered, unzipped, stood there, and held my breath.

After about forty-five seconds I felt the tension in my chest for lack of breath, and I wanted to gasp . . . My brain—in fact, my whole body—was telling me to *breathe!* I started to have second thoughts about doing this at 36,000 feet. But I talked myself into waiting there a little longer . . .

. . . *VOILA!* My bladder muscle released, and I urinated in an airplane lavatory for the first time in more years than I could remember. I almost cried with happiness. I was literally on cloud nine.

As I exited the lavatory, I thought about high-fiving the flight attendant to celebrate. But it stayed a thought. I didn't want to end up on the nightly news.

The Casino

I landed in Las Vegas and was excited about the possibilities of experimenting with using public bathrooms in and around the Convention Center. They say practice makes perfect, and with paruresis recovery, this is particularly important!

Prior to this moment, using a casino bathroom would be one of the scariest things I could think of trying. But with my newfound confidence (of which I was still a little skeptical), I was eager to try.

I checked in at my hotel then walked through the casino (by the way, I don't gamble, but these conventions are always in hotels with casinos). Eventually I stepped into the bathroom, which was busy. I gave it a try . . . but it didn't work. I knew I was nervous, and probably still a little skeptical that breath holding would work every time. This was a different scenario than the airplane, where I was the only one in the bathroom. In this case, there were people around and I started to get self conscious about standing there for what I thought was too long. So I gave up and started breathing, zipped up and walked away.

I thought "Oh, well," and just shrugged it off. After walking around the casino some more I decided to give it another go.

Bingo. It worked. I just had to hold my breath a little longer.

This wasn't easy; my body really wanted to breathe, and I even started gasping for air a little. But I think because I'm a competitive swimmer, I knew I wasn't going to die if I held my breath a bit more. In the back of my mind I was thinking it wouldn't be ideal if I passed out and hit my head, but in the end I felt it was worth trying . . . So I held my breath about ten or fifteen seconds longer and, again, it worked! I had urinated in a public bathroom, in a urinal, with other men standing near me.

Holy moly! I thought, exhilarated. *I might be on to something here!*

Fluid-Loading

The next day was the first day of the convention. Normally at a time like this I wouldn't drink anything, even coffee (well, okay, maybe a little coffee . . . I need my coffee). But I decided to do something different: I had a couple of glasses of water and a normal cup of coffee.

Experts say that fluid intake is important; they call it "fluid loading." And then, for people with paruresis, it's best to wait until your bladder is at a 7 or above on a 1-10 scale of "How badly do I have to go?" Some people living with paruresis urinate much more frequently than "normal." This is probably because we don't want to miss the opportunity to "go," as we don't know when we'll find a safe place to urinate. So we head to the bathroom frequently because we're anticipating not being able to go at some point during the day. The problem with this is we aren't following the normal rhythm of how our bladder is supposed to operate. We don't learn what having a full bladder really feels like. It's kind of a paradox.

Of course, it's also true that paruresis sufferers may go *less* often, especially when a "safe" bathroom isn't available. Here too we are over-riding our body's natural rhythm.

Anyway, I fluid-loaded the morning of the first day of the convention, and when it came time to use the busy public bathroom I walked right up to the urinal, did the breath-holding technique, and it worked again! And it continued to work every time I went to the bathroom that day!

From Anxiety to Excitement

That night there was a reception at The Sphere theater in Las

Vegas, with thousands of people attending. Rather than getting anxious and nervous—which I usually was before going to a crowded place like that with no private bathrooms—I was excited to try out the facilities there. This was a new experience for me. Just a few weeks prior, I would have spent a lot of time thinking about all of the scenarios around whether I would be able to find a safe place to pee at the event. Not this time. This time I was able to be present and enjoy the immersive experience that The Sphere is famous for. I walked around the venue as we waited for the show to start, checking out the high-tech gadgets and robots that were on display. I even waited in line to experience a virtual-reality show. And I drank a bottle of water, not worrying about what would happen when my bladder got full.

Which, before long it did. And lo and behold, I was able to go again. This time I noticed something quite amazing: I was able to urinate at a public urinal with many other people around—without holding my breath. It occurred to me that I was relaxing enough to go in a situation I had never been able to go in before. It was as if my knowing I could go if I held my breath somehow made me relax enough to go *without* holding my breath.

This was a huge revelation for me. I had heard of this phenomenon happening with people who use self-catheterization. It is a kind of shifting of reality of what the brain is believing, almost as if the brain is saying, "Well, he's gonna be able to go anyway, so we might as well just open the floodgates." I was amazed to experience this for myself. (And it started to make me wonder where else in my life I was holding onto beliefs that weren't serving me.)

Noticing

The rest of my time in Vegas was extremely enjoyable and, frankly, a little unbelievable to me. I was completely transformed and felt like a huge weight had been lifted from my shoulders. I even started to have fun trying to find bathrooms where I *couldn't* go pee! It only happened once . . . and then I went back shortly after and was able to go.

I also noticed I was starting to be way more present when urinating. For example, prior to this I spent all of my time in the bathroom worried about not being able to pee. The worry would start even before I went into the bathroom—basically from the moment I started to feel pressure on my bladder as it started to fill. This worried thinking would often consume me and interfere with whatever else I was trying to focus on. The future became a big, scary unknown based on my frustrated thinking about past unsuccessful attempts to pee in public.

All in all, it was a vicious cycle of unhealthy thinking. But now, I was starting to be aware of my surroundings in the moment, and of the act of peeing, and noticing it without the negative thinking. Noticing the feeling of relaxing as I voided into the urinal . . . Noticing the noise that I made when hitting different sections of the urinal . . . the ceramic, the water, or the plastic urinal screen.

One of the other cool things I noticed was that other men have no interest in what I am or am not doing in the bathroom.

For years I've created stories in my head such as:

- "I wonder if he's noticing how long I'm standing here?"
- "I wonder if anyone is noticing that I'm not urinating yet?"
- "I wonder if anyone is noticing how noisy (or quiet) I'm

being?"

You get the picture. But as my mind started to relax—regardless of the fact that I was standing in front of a urinal—I gradually realized that *nobody cares about me at all* when they're occupied with their own business. They only care about themselves.

We could even extend that concept beyond the bathroom in terms of how everyone is wrapped up in their own thinking as they go about their lives. But we'll pick up that idea in a later chapter.

On my way home I drank a large coffee and an orange juice just before my flight. I was determined to test my newfound ability to pee on a plane. I did not fail to do so; in fact, I ended up urinating twice in that airplane lavatory. At the connecting airport I even drank a large Jamba Juice. A "liquid lunch" would have been inconceivable only a few months before. But I no longer feared going to the bathroom. In fact, I looked forward to it.

15.

The In-Person Workshop

Shortly after arriving home from Las Vegas, I was scheduled to attend my first in-person workshop sponsored by the International Paruresis Association. Honestly, I wasn't sure I really needed it after my great successes during my trip to Las Vegas. But I remembered from my conversation with Tim Pyle that he has attended many workshops and picked up something new each time. So, I decided to go.

A Star of Stage and Screen

I also knew this workshop was being recorded by one of the attendees as part of a documentary he was working on to bring public awareness to shy bladder/paruresis. Because of this, attendees signed a release allowing us to be recorded—or not. The waiver had various options: not to be filmed, to only be filmed from behind or certain other angles, or without restriction. Unusually for me, I felt very willing to put myself out there, and volunteered to be recorded without restrictions. It felt important to help the documentary makers and hopefully other people watching the future production. So I signed the release form, they mic'd me up, and I was ready to "go." I told myself that if I could go pee in front of a camera, then I could go anywhere/anytime! And pee in front of a camera I did (from behind), which is not the acting debut I had envisioned for myself, but it was a rewarding experience nonetheless.

No Breath Holding

The workshop was scheduled to begin Friday night and run through most of the day on Sunday. I was a little nervous; I knew there would be alot of practicing with a partner. But I was also excited. I hadn't lost the glow of enthusiasm from my experience in Las Vegas. I was going into this workshop a new man, essentially, and it felt like I was continuing an adventure I'd just started.

I was also curious what the outcome would be. Would this workshop help me in ways I hadn't considered yet? I had signed up when starting my recovery journey because I'm the type of person who jumps into things 100 percent, and there happened to be three events I could sign up for, all happening within the first month (the support group, the virtual workshop and now the in-person workshop). I did like the idea of meeting other men like me in person to share my story and hear theirs. Thus far, all my interactions with the IPA community had been virtual. I was looking forward to getting to know some of my fellow paruretics.

When I arrived on Friday night, I pulled aside the famous Dr. Steven Soifer—one of the workshop leaders—and told him of my recent success. He was very supportive of my still attending, and he suggested that I focus on working on graduated exposure and try not to use the breath-holding technique over the weekend. Not that there was anything wrong with breath holding. The workshop leaders encourage members to try different techniques, tools, therapies, tricks, and even some doctor-prescribed pharmaceuticals that have been shown to be helpful, to see what works best for them. This workshop, though, was heavily focused on graduated exposure. As we would be pairing up with a pee buddy to practice gradually exposing ourselves to more difficult situations, I thought it was a great idea to use the same technique as my buddy, so I decided not to use the breath-holding technique that weekend.

Sharing

Friday night was spent meeting the group—all men who were suffering with paruresis. We shared our stories, which were varied but uniformly emotional. Each of us had developed ways to live and cope with a shy bladder. Many, like me, had been doing so for decades. We all had unique reasons for attending as well, aside from simply wanting to learn more and cure the condition. One man had a goal of flying across the world to attend a wedding. Another wanted to keep a job as it transitioned from "work from home" to "back to the office" after the pandemic. Most men had either told no one or very few people about their condition.

One thing I noticed was that a kind of lightness came over people as they told their stories. I know I felt this myself as I shared, even though I had done so before.

Saturday and Sunday were in large part educational. In sessions led by Steven Soifer, Ph.D., MSW, and Dan Rocker, LCSW, MA.,[5] the program included everything from a history of paruresis

---

[5] Both Steven and Dan are co-Directors of the IPA's Shy Bladder Center and IPA Shy Bladder Center therapists.

research and the IPA, the anatomy of the bladder, some information about anxiety and thinking around the topic of shy bladder, and goal-setting as it related to what each person was looking for out of the workshop.

Graduated Exposure

The other part of the workshop involved practice-peeing with a partner, which we did throughout the day. This sounded very strange at first, but it turned out to be extremely rewarding. We had been fluid-loading, so I really had to pee. This made going much easier. The challenge though, was that we had to stop our flow after about three seconds. This was so that we would still have a strong urge to go as we gradually moved to more scary or uncomfortable situations.

Following the steps of the graduated exposure technique, we started with what was most comfortable for each of us. For me, this was having my partner stand near the hotel bed, while I tried peeing in the hotel bathroom with the door closed. Then we gradually moved into more uncomfortable areas. For me this was having my partner stand in the hotel bathroom with me while I attempted to pee. The last example mimicked what standing at a urinal would be like.

I realized early in the workshop that I now had no hesitation peeing in any scenario I put myself in. Whether it was with my partner in the hotel room bathroom, or in the lobby bathroom downstairs. Even when we all walked to the mall next-door, I was able to pee without holding my breath. This was an interesting experience for me, having had so much success with the breath-holding technique in Las Vegas. I was excited, yet curious as to why

I didn't have to use the breath-holding technique at all. Graduated exposure was working for me to the point where I reached my hardest exposure goal, which was peeing at a urinal at a busy mall bathroom, located right off the food court. It was a huge bathroom, and very busy. Men and boys of all ages were entering and leaving the bathroom and I wasn't fazed in the least. I was able to pee every time I tried.

New Relationships

I also got into quite deep conversations with my pee buddies over the weekend. For much of the weekend I was paired with Steven Jackson and his camera crew, who were shooting a documentary called *Pee Shy*, which chronicles Steven's own personal journey of living with Shy Bladder Syndrome. Steven and I got into deep conversations, as he wanted to document what we were thinking as we went through the graduated exposure exercise. I found this to be interesting and rewarding because I got to reflect in real time about how I was feeling as I found myself peeing in every situation I tried to go. It was amazing, liberating, refreshing and exciting—with a little bit of anxiety all wrapped into one. Not only was I having a new, life-changing experience, I was also sharing it with my pee buddy, his film crew, and probably the world (when the documentary is ultimately released).

A huge part of the weekend was spent developing relationships with some amazing, courageous men who are likely to become lifelong friends. I feel like I am now part of a special fraternity. A few of us went out for dinner Saturday night and got to know each other on a more personal level. And I've stayed in touch with quite a few more. Some of us have even started "pee practicing" together locally and have been meeting regularly with an in-person support group I've organized in Portland, Maine.

It was also amazing to meet and talk with both Steve and Dan, who were wonderful workshop facilitators. They structured the whole weekend to be at everyone's pace and comfort level, and they excelled at making the group feel comfortable, regardless of the severity of individual participants' conditions and the anxiety they felt about the weekend. This was confirmed for me at the end of the workshop, when we were asked to give one word that described their experience. These words were all positive, and everyone seemed to have progressed towards recovery at some level during the weekend.

Overall, I can't recommend the IPA-sponsored workshops enough for people suffering with paruresis. For me, they are part of the process that has changed my life.

IV: Navigating the Shy Bladder Recovery Journey

Mindset and Techniques

16.

My Major Insight

We Live in an Inside-Out Reality

In 2019 I had an insight that changed my life. I'm going to share the insight and understanding here, not because you have to understand any of the concepts in order to overcome paruresis (you don't), but because they have been so helpful to me on my own journey—particularly in helping me understand my thinking around my shy bladder—and I think they can help anyone who is open to them.

In 2019 I read a book by Michael Neill called *The Inside-Out Revolution*, and at some point during the book I realized that my experience of life is 100 percent created by my own thinking in the moment. One-hundred percent. Not 70 percent, 80 percent, 90 percent . . . but 100 percent generated by my thinking. It was a "hand-smack-to-my-forehead," life-changing moment when I saw clearly that my experiences were not being created by circumstances (outside-in), but strictly by my thinking and the meaning I was creating about things (inside-out).[6]

At this time in my life I was in the process of leaving a job I really enjoyed because I had been too sick to keep up the heavy travel and workload. I was miserable, anxious, and depressed, and I blamed my woes on the fact that I had to resign from my job. It was a low point in my life, and I was blaming a lot of things "outside of me" on the way I felt.

This was a typical habit of mine up until that point in my life. I thought if I could just change things on the outside I would feel better. For much of my life this meant changing jobs or careers. I was really good at that, and managed to create and maintain several different successful careers. But none of them made me happy, like I thought they would. In fact, quite the opposite: I would succeed at my job or business, but because I was in low moods, anxious and even depressed at times, I would later decide I needed to change jobs.

In other words, I tried to fix the way I felt by changing my circumstances (job).

What I came to realize is that the only thing that can change the way I feel is how I *respond* to my own thinking.

This was a powerful realization for me. I had been a student of self-help techniques up until that point, having read dozens of books, watched videos, attended courses, and invested a lot of time and money in trying to improve my thinking. In trying to change or fix my thinking. And many of these techniques seemed to work, at least for a while.

---

[6] Neill's book was based on the teachings of Sydney Banks, who discovered a new set of psychological principles, which are known as The Three Principles of Mind, Consciousness and Thought, or often just The Three Principles, in the early 1970s. (You can read more about Sydney Banks and his work in Appendix I.)

What I realized in 2019, when I had my insight about how life *really* works, is that there is absolutely nothing to fix! I realized I was "whole" the way I was, and that anytime I felt out of synch, this feeling was being generated by believing my thinking in the moment. And that the wonderful part of it all was that there was nothing to do about it. Thoughts are fluid. They come and go, and only become real when we give them energy—that is, when we focus on them, acting and responding to them as if they are real. Try as we might, we can't work our way out of messy thinking. I learned that if I just leave my thoughts alone, my thinking will clear out on its own, in its own time.

Still Water, Clear Water

A great example of how this works is to imagine yourself on vacation, playing in the ocean at your favorite beach on a beautiful, windy day. The waves are rolling in, pounding the sand and causing a lot of whitewater. One of your favorite vacation pastimes is looking for seashells. As you wade out into the water you decide to dive under to look for shells. As you open your eyes all you can see is a white and bluish-gray blur. You can't make out anything clearly, and it's even hard to see your hand as you hold it out in front of you. You know the shells are down there, but everything is just so messy. No matter how hard you try to see through the "noise" of the water, you just can't see the shells.

Fast-forward a few days and the wind has died down, and consequently the rough seas have grown calm. You decide to try your luck now and see if the water has cleared. As you wade out, you notice the clarity of the water. You can see the bottom clearly as you tiptoe through the sand. Eventually, you duck your head under and open your eyes. Today is a much different experience; you can see clearly for quite a distance! And the beautiful shells are everywhere, in many different shapes and colors.

What is interesting is that the shells have always been there—you just weren't able to see them clearly. The only thing you had to do was wait it out until the water calmed down. Now, if a few days earlier, you had tried to somehow "clear" the turbulent water, this would have been an exercise in futility. You can't change Mother Nature, and in my experience you can't force your thoughts to change either!

Here's what I'm getting at: there are times when our thoughts are so turbulent we can't see clearly. My own experience with job-switching is just one illustration of that. Many others exist in our daily lives—for example, when we take a bad day at work home with us and get into an argument with our spouses, or if someone cuts us off on the highway and we get riled up and (hopefully only momentarily) think that chasing after them is a good idea.

When our thinking is turbulent, it impacts how we experience what's happening around us and the decisions we make. When this happens, our job isn't to *make* our thinking less turbulent—it's to give it the space to "peter out" so that we once again come from a place of inner wisdom. There's a reason why the phrase "think clearly" came into common use.

When we start to live from the understanding that our own thinking, and not our circumstances, creates our experience of reality, it becomes easier not to get caught up in the turbulence of thought. This leads to a deeper sense of inner calm, clearer thinking, and a more peaceful experience of life. The paradox is that you can't "try" to get to that clear thinking, but it's always there under the mental noise.

What Does This Have to Do with Shy Bladder?

In my case, once I started to understand how thought operates in my life, my thinking began to change. For example I used to create a lot of meaning around the fact that I couldn't urinate at a urinal. This led to my quitting trying after only about fifteen to twenty seconds—which seemed like three to four minutes back then. I'd tell myself stories like, "These other men must be thinking I'm standing here too long"—and I would *believe* these stories. I would believe my thinking and react by getting even more self-conscious about going. So my experience of shy bladder was fraught with frustration to the point of trauma. (This despite the fact that I'm sure other men had more important things to think about. And by some strange chance, even if they *were* thinking about it, what's that to me?)

But as my thinking changed, so did my experience. I've shared my Vegas experience with breath-holding, and how this led me to see that soon I didn't even need to hold my breath to go. I've let go of the thinking that people are paying attention to me when I'm at the urinal. Now I look at bathroom situations more like a game. They are fun. I've changed my experience from one of fear and dread to one of possibility. Every time I enter a restroom, I think about how fun it is that I can stand up at a urinal without fear. And in the cases where I can't urinate, for whatever reason, I walk away and don't create any meaning about it. I'll just try again later. Turning it into a game is still *thinking*, but it's more fun and—more importantly, perhaps—*it works*.

Our Thinking Is Neutral

I've come to realize that the stories we tell ourselves and the meaning we give to those stories varies from moment to moment. We, as the thinkers, can decide what meaning we assign to our thinking. Sometimes our thinking is negative, sometimes it's positive—depending on the meaning we make up about it in the moment. Furthermore, that meaning can change depending on our mood. What seems like a negative thought in a low mood, might take a positive spin when we're in a better mood. When we're in a particularly good mood we might even laugh at how strange life can be when we can't accomplish something we can normally do—such as when, for some reason, I can't go even in a place where I've gone before. When such a thing happens, I could give it the meaning that something's gone wrong and I'm going to have to struggle to make sure I can go next time. Or I can simply try again later.

The coolest thing about all of this is that there is absolutely nothing to do about any of it—other than to notice our thinking. Positive or negative thinking is not intrinsically good or bad; it just is. It's completely neutral until we make meaning about it. And the act of noticing it, of being aware of our thinking—eventually brings us back to a neutral state. Just like waiting for the ocean to calm down enables us to see clearly under water.

And this is where the magic happens. In this neutral space, unclouded by overthinking, we are open to new thought.

If you've read this far, I encourage you to play with this concept, perhaps even reread the chapter and consider how this understanding might apply to your own life. Maybe ask yourself things like,

- Where in your life can you consider waiting for the "water" to clear?
- What might you see, or not see?
- What might happen if you didn't try as hard to fix things?
- What would be true for you if there were nothing to "fix"?

If none of this "clicks" at the moment, that's fine. It didn't at first for me either; it took some time sitting with it, reading, learning and sharing more. It's not something that you have to "get" right away, or even at all! I'm sharing it because it's been helpful in my journey with shy bladder, and in many other areas of my life, and I hope that it might be in yours as well.

17.

Other Ways My Life Has Improved

Since learning and studying The Three Principles I've realized some amazing accomplishments in addition to overcoming paruresis. My understanding of the nature of thought is a major reason why. Here are a few of the accomplishments, which, interestingly, I have not "tried" to achieve. They simply happened as I gained a deeper understanding of the fact that my own thinking is the driving force behind how my experience is created.

Anxiety and OCD

I have a history of living with, and suffering from, different levels of anxiety and tendencies that lean towards Obsessive Compulsive Disorder (OCD) throughout my life. I have experienced the feeling across a wide spectrum of anxiousness, from being mildly annoying to debilitating at times. For me, anxious feelings range from a light tightness in my chest on the low end, to feelings of dread and wanting to cry, not being able to focus on anything, and insomnia. I have even contemplated suicide on the high end. I've never been diagnosed with OCD but I'm pretty sure I have it. Reflecting on what I've learned about OCD behavior, I definitely have issues. At times in the past this included repetitively checking that I locked the car as well as some ruminative tendencies— meaning an inability to escape the grip of my own thinking.

For example, as a new parent of two toddlers in my early twenties, I ran one of my family's car dealerships. I pushed myself hard to succeed at the job and suffered significant stress—to the degree where at one point I found myself curled up in a ball on my sofa, unable to move, feeling helpless, alone, defeated, stuck . . . and not knowing what do to do to fix the spinning in my head. I was physically ill and mentally drained. I stayed that way in my mind for what seems like days. It was a very low place.

I didn't know how to separate work and family life, especially because my father would often bring family into work and work into family. It was what we did in our family. Gatherings were spent talking mostly about the car business. Without going into all the details, I'll simply say it was a perfect storm that resulted in sleepless nights and coping with my stress and anxiety by excessive drinking, eating and not taking care of myself.

At the time I didn't understand the impact that my thinking had on my reality. I didn't understand that my stress and anxiety was caused simply by believing all the thoughts I was thinking. Stress wasn't caused by circumstances, work, work-life balance, or anything "out there." Instead, stress lay in how I thought about— and subsequently reacted to—all of those things. If I thought it was "bad" that I worked at the family dealership, it was bad. If I thought this was the only thing I was good at, and the only way I could make a decent living, that was my reality. It was the meaning I had been placing on those things that was creating my experience. My low moods made it worse in a vicious-cycle kind of way. I innocently didn't see this at the time.

One consequence was that I decided to quit the family business. By the time I was twenty-seven I was running two car dealerships and sick to my stomach with anxiety most of the time. I believed that changing careers would make me happy. I became a stockbroker with Smith Barney. But that didn't make me happy. I was stressed out and anxious because I wasn't making enough money to support my family. Also, I was anxious all the time about managing other people's investments. So I left that job and became an executive recruiter, with the promise of making a lot of money. I thrived at that job for a while, made a lot more money, and became a top sales producer in record time. But that job didn't make me happy either. The market turned, my income dropped, and once again I was miserable.

I even believed that if we moved it would help me feel better. So we did—we moved from Maine to Florida. I made up excuses that we were doing it to help grow my new business, which I had just started. My business partner lived in Florida, so moving made sense on paper. But underneath it all was my belief that if we moved, I would feel better. And even be healthier because we could be outside all year round! We could walk outside every day, swim, go golfing, lie on the beach!

Yet despite some amazing experiences there, I was still anxious and overwhelmed in Florida. I wasn't sleeping well, I gained weight and we started getting into debt. I blamed everything on my business, which had been robust, but which was now experiencing struggles . . . but really it was my mindset, which was very victim-based at the time.

At any rate, all of these experiences were infused with

anxiety and OCD, both of which impacted the decisions I made and my experience of life. Today, I understand that my experience with anxiety and OCD is different, in a good way. I don't have the same mental chatter that I did even a few years ago that leads to significant anxiety or obsessive-compulsive behavior. I believe this is because I've learned how my thinking works, and this has led to the realization that I am the creator of the meaning I give to my thoughts. I can decide to believe those thoughts or not. To use an example from earlier in the book, I can decide whether to believe the thought that the guy standing next to me at the urinal *must* be thinking about how long it's taking me to go. I can decide whether to believe it would even matter if he *did* think that. I can decide to believe my thinking that the only way to escape my anxious thinking around a job is to quit. And so on.

Thoughts, in and of themselves, are neutral. I have the power to make any given thought real by "inflating" it with my belief.

Alcohol

I gave up drinking alcohol and have not had a drink for over six years. I don't believe I was an alcoholic (then again, most alcoholics don't), but I know I did not have a healthy relationship with alcohol. I drank as a coping mechanism to help with my anxiety (which was strongly connected to my paruresis). I've always had a tendency (and at times, more than a tendency) to be anxious.

I have always been an overthinker. My mind is so busy that it is exhausting, and this is a source of anxiety. I have tried many things to help over the years, including prescription medication, professional therapy, meditation, swimming and other athletic endeavors. Alcohol was an easy way to cope. It was accessible and seemed to work. But it always made things worse. I made bad decisions when I was drinking. It affected my overall health. I often woke up hungover and unable to function at a hundred percent. I didn't think clearly, and I know it affected my relationship with my wife and daughters.

I tried to give it up in the past, but after a year and a half of not drinking, I landed a new job that required me to attend and host dinners for our business clients. I convinced myself that I needed to drink to fit in and make others comfortable. (I realize now that this was just a made-up story I was telling myself; I did not really need to drink.)

In July of 2019, around the same time I found The Three Principles, I gave up alcohol for good and have not had a drink since. Today, I have completely changed my reality from feeling I need to drink to reduce my anxiety, to a foundation of *not* drinking because it will help me live a long, healthy life. As I started to live my life without alcohol, I discovered I was more productive, and I was thinking more clearly. I realized that nobody cares if I drink or not. Social acceptance was one of the stories I had chosen to believe about drinking. I felt that people would judge me for not drinking in a social setting. Thankfully, my thinking changed, and my experience followed. I do not miss drinking at all. I feel empowered by a positive lifestyle choice that I have 100 percent control over.

Financial Freedom

Another huge accomplishment is that my wife and I reduced our debt by over $100,000. As a result of an illness, some ill-timed job changes, and some poor financial decisions, we were deep in debt. Looking back on it, it's amazing to me the stories we tell ourselves about money. For example, I believed that spending money on things could help me feel better. A luxury car, a big house on a golf course, brand-name clothes, a country club membership.

The truth is that nothing outside of me can make me feel anything. Only my *thinking* about it can make me feel something. I have found this to be true with my career as well. In the past I've made rash decisions to leave a job or change direction with my business. Although these have all worked out for me, some of the decisions resulted in going into more debt.

I feel fortunate to have learned how our minds work, and it has resulted in me making much better financial decisions over the past five years. Today, we have no credit card debt, no personal loans, and our college loan debts are almost paid off. We also now have a nice savings account, which we have not always had. My understanding of the Three Principles helped me to create a different reality about work and money. I realized I was creating stories around how spending money made me feel good. That going out for coffee made me feel a certain way. Or that it was a good idea to buy an item I didn't really need in order to get a rush of happiness (which would only last a few minutes).

So, we started to create different stories and habits via our thoughts. Old habits can be replaced by new habits. It just takes the decision to stop the old habit and replace it with a new one. *And* to recognize the old-habit thinking—which will still enter the brain—for what it is: just a thought. It's not something I have to give energy to. In the case of my wife and me, our new stories and habits revolve around wanting to invest our money, around the powerful feeling of having money in the bank. Having a nice cushion. Of being happy, regardless of what I'm doing for work. There's probably a separate book here about how we accomplished this, but behind it all was our understanding of the Three Principles.

Recovery from Lyme Disease

The Three Principles understanding has also helped me create a different experience around my health. In 2018 I was diagnosed with chronic Lyme disease and was forced to resign from a job I really loved because I could not handle the intense workload and travel. This was a devastating period for me. I was traveling for weeks at a time and running mastermind / process-improvement meetings for business owners all around North America. I would often spend all day flying to a West Coast city, such as Vancouver, B.C., then run a two-to-three day meeting. I would also host the group dinner, which typically ran into the wee hours of the morning (for my brain, anyway, which was on East Coast time).

The job required late nights and early mornings, and a need for me to be "on" with few breaks during the day. It was a challenging schedule even for someone in great health—and I was not healthy. Add to this the fact that I couldn't fall asleep consistently, so my sleep deprivation just compounded my overall lousy feelings all the time. I was constantly exhausted; I picked up a nervous twitch, had brain fog and body pain, and generally thought I was going to die.

Oh, and I had a shy bladder, and trying to find bathrooms I could safely use during these meetings was on my mind all the time.

Thankfully, the amazing support of my wife, combined with my learning/studying the Three Principles, led me to seek out an amazing medical team and other healing resources to help me recover. I believe my understanding of the Three Principles facilitated my willingness to seek out and engage with approaches I wouldn't have considered otherwise. I have found that when my mind is calm, I am open to new ideas. In this case, my calm mind helped me be open to working with a chiropractor, who pointed me in different directions to get more help. For example, I discovered a naturopath who took the time to listen to me, make recommendations, review tests . . . and listen to me even more. I found an acupuncturist who has been an unwavering advocate for me, an invaluable resource to me and my family, and a great friend. I also discovered and became a patient of a brilliant primary care physician who sees the whole individual, and not just a patient. He has taken time to get to know me and my wants and needs. In the past I had not really been open to alternative medical treatments. I believed that by seeking out "experts" in the medical field, I would find my answers. This usually led to expensive medical procedures, like MRIs and CAT scans, to help figure out what was "wrong" with me. While good at eliminating major causes known by the scientific world, these traditional tests and therapies (like anxiety prescriptions), didn't help me. By looking within I started to believe I could heal myself, and this led me down the less traditional approach of working with my medical team as partners, rather than directors, in my journey of healing. In other words, I have a powerful healthcare team, and I know they always have my back—all which has led me to have fully recovered from chronic Lyme disease.

Coaching

Lastly, since I've been making better decisions operating from a clear and present mind, I started a coaching business where I help people see the resilience and wisdom within them, to help them change their experience of living with stress, overwhelm, chronic pain and anxiety. I've helped hundreds of people transform their lives, and the lives of those around them, by pointing them to the power of their inner wisdom. I've had many people tell me how their own lives have been transformed after I helped them see the stories they're telling themselves—and believing—and how they are now having insights for themselves. I share a little more about the coaching process in an appendix at the end of the book.

18.

Breath Holding

The breath-holding technique was instrumental in helping me recover from primary paruresis. It was probably my single most important discovery. This is why I'm devoting an entire chapter to it. Throughout this book I've shared some background and my personal experiences with other valuable techniques for paruresis, such as graduated exposure. But because of my personal experiences and success with the breath-holding technique, it makes sense to share some more details of my story in the hopes that it will support people who wish to consider it.

So in this chapter I'll share some of the research that points to what's behind the technique's effectiveness. I will also explore in detail how I've successfully used the technique, and how my thoughts about urinating in public have changed since then.

I do want to stress the need to discuss your practice of this technique with your physician. I discuss some of the pros and cons of the practice in this chapter, but everyone is different, and it is important to get input specific to your particular needs from a trusted health professional.

I first read about the breath-holding technique in *The Secret*

Social Phobia: Shy Blader Syndrome (Paruresis): Second Edition. This was early on in my recovery efforts. The book discusses how psychologist Dr. Monroe Weil originally championed the technique.[7] When I attended my initial shy bladder support group, IPA Board Member and group leader David Kliss talked about his success in using the technique. In order to understand further what it was all about, I later watched a video interview in which Kliss describes how to perform the technique (a link to the video is in the Resources section at the back of this book).

Why does it work? Research reported in the book *Breath: The New Science of a Lost Art,* by James Nestor, points to breath holding as an effective technique to help people who suffer from anxiety by specifically altering the levels of carbon dioxide and oxygen in the body. Nestor points out that many breath-holding therapies "have been around for thousands of years."[8] He shares data from studies designed to help people get over their anxieties by increasing their levels of carbon dioxide—whether through holding one's breath or, more aggressively, by inhaling puffs of carbon dioxide. The increase in carbon dioxide seems to trigger a fear response—"the deep fear and crushing anxiety that comes from the feeling of not being able to take another breath"[9]—that paradoxically then helps reduce or eliminate anxiety.

In terms of shy bladder, it seems quite possible to me that the anxiety and fear related to not being able to breathe over-rides the anxiety around urinating. It's as if the brain says, "I've got bigger fish to fry!" and releases the sphincter muscles.

---

[7] Soifer, S., *Zgourides*, G. D., Himle, J., & O'Brien, N. (2020). *The Secret Social Phobia: Shy bladder syndrome (paruresis): Second Edition.* International Paruresis Association, Inc., 134-136.

[8] Nestor, J. (2021). *Breath: The new science of a lost art.* Penguin Life, 174.

[9] *Ibid.,* 169.

After doing my research, I set out to try breath holding on my own. I figured "I'm a competitive swimmer; I'm used to holding my breath." So I was confident that if anyone could succeed at this technique, I could. I've talked in previous chapters about my different attempts, misfires and successes as I learned how to perfect the breath-holding technique. Today, I am able to void in any situation I have tried using the breath-holding technique, including busy airport restrooms with lines of men waiting behind me.

What I learned in my experimenting with breath holding is that although it's not hard to do, it can be quite uncomfortable. Also, in my case (and I suspect for others as well, based on many conversations with paruresis sufferers), I had to deal with my mind making up stories around the process—before, during and after. I'll explain more about this below.

But first, the following is a step-by-step explanation of how I had success using the breath-holding technique.

Step 1: I realized I was believing my thinking, so I changed what I thought and believed

The first thing I did was tell myself that breath holding was going to work. I believed it in every cell in my body. When I first heard about it, I couldn't believe something so seemingly simple could work—even though I knew someone for whom it had (David Kliss). But I came to realize that here was a solution that worked for many people. So I started ignoring the habitual thinking that told me I could not urinate in a public bathroom, and started believing that breath holding would work for me. More than that, I *knew* it would work for me.

Step 2: I practiced breath holding in typically stressful or "unsafe" situations

This sounds counterintuitive, but it comes from my own experience.

I first tried breath holding in a Walmart bathroom. Normally that would be a great place to practice as my brain would typically consider it "unsafe." But on the first day I tried, the bathroom was empty. I was able to void, but I don't believe in this case that breath holding was the factor. Feeling that this was a "safe" environment was the primary factor in my being able to void in the bathroom. I knew this for sure because of my next attempt: on a five-hour flight from Baltimore to Las Vegas. I was two hours into the flight and really had to go to the bathroom. Earlier in this book I described a similar situation just weeks before in which I was completely unable to go and had to sit in extreme discomfort until the flight landed. At that time my mind obviously considered the airplane bathroom "unsafe," and my brain locked up my sphincter muscles. This time, however, I held my breath and went.

Step 3: I held my breath until I felt I couldn't. And kept holding it.

In my experience, I need to hold my breath until my body starts trying to take breaths on its own. It seems a little like a gasp reflex is taking over. I get a little light-headed. Then I keep holding my breath a little longer. I fight the urge to breathe and ignore the stories my thoughts are telling me—such as, "Breathe, you idiot! You're going to pass out!"

I was curious about the safety of breath holding in general, as I've always been fascinated with people who use breath holding to dive for long periods of time. I loved the movie *My Octopus Teacher*, a documentary that followed the story of filmmaker Craig Foster's year-long interaction with an octopus off the coast of South Africa. It was so cool that he was able to free dive without an oxygen tank for long periods of time. That has been a dream of mine and something I'd love to train to do.

I mention this because, based on my research, the general conclusion is that for healthy people, there are no serious risks to holding one's breath in the time it would take for breath holding to work for paruresis. Which, in my experience, at the beginning of my recovery, was somewhere between 60-90 seconds.

The most serious side effects that researchers find, and that I've personally experienced, are dizziness, lightheadedness, breath hunger and, on occasion, headaches. And I don't know if it's considered a side effect or not, but it can be embarrassing if I am believing my thoughts that anyone near me is paying attention to what I'm doing. Perhaps they can hear my lungs gasping for breath? Or perhaps they know how long I've been standing at the urinal? I know it's just a story I'm telling myself, but it can be real in the moment, and it has the potential to make me take a breath before the technique has a chance to work.

One particular article I read[10] suggested that people can hold their breath for up to 60 seconds without falling into trouble. Additionally, it suggested, that it's probably safe for up to 90 seconds. Beyond that and you risk passing out, which can cause you to hit your head or break a bone. Also, the article mentions that "The heart muscle is very sensitive to oxygen, and just a few minutes

---

[10] https://health.osu.edu/health/general-health/what-happens-when-you-hold-your-breath

without oxygen can lead to a heart attack." Therefore, if you have a heart condition you should not try this technique. (And as always, please check with your physician before trying this technique.)

Step 4: I ignored my "gasp" reflex—aka my intense desire to BREATHE

In the beginning of my practicing this technique, I would typically hold my breath for sixty to ninety seconds before I started to void. As a long-term swimmer, I know I can hold my breath for that long, and even much longer if I need to. So I know *intellectually* that I can hold my breath. But my body's instinct is to breathe, so it's easy to believe the stories that come into my head during the process and the inner command to just give in and breathe.

The key for me has been to ignore what I call the "gasp reflex." That's perhaps not the correct terminology, but it's how I describe the feeling I have when my upper stomach area is convulsing, begging me to breath. I have found that ignoring this request for about ten to fifteen seconds is what leads to the next step.

Step 5: I enjoy the flow

Almost immediately after I ignore the gasp reflex, my bladder muscles relax and I void without trying. This has worked in every situation in which I've tried it. Airplane lavatories, airport restrooms, concert venues, convention centers and even busy casinos. One trick I've learned is to hold my breath a few seconds beyond when I start the flow. There's something about doing this that maintains a consistent flow when I start to breathe.

And breathe we must at this time. I'm just careful not to gasp or inhale air too quickly. I try to calmly take my first breath and just breathe normally as I empty my bladder. I do this so as not to draw attention to myself by making weird noises. It's easy for me to start believing the thoughts I have that other people can hear my gasping for that first breath. I know they can't, but it sure seems like it in the moment.

Since I've started using this technique, some interesting things have happened. First, I've found that I don't have to use it any longer, in most situations. For example, I was at a convention recently and was able to use a moderately busy men's room, standing at the urinal, without holding my breath. I can also void in airplane lavatories, most of the time without holding my breath.

Second, I've found that I don't have to hold my breath as long as I did when first learning the technique. It's almost as if my brain says, "Okay, I get it. You're using the breath-holding technique. We're just going to release the muscle now and not fight you." I believe that the breath-holding technique has helped retrain my brain's belief of what defines a "safe" or "unsafe" bathroom environment. What was completely unsafe a year ago, such as using a urinal in a casino restroom, is now an experience I actually look forward to.

As an interesting sidenote, have you ever experienced something similar? What I want people to understand is that in my case and others, once you learn this and other techniques, you probably won't have to rely on them for the rest of your life. I've learned this technique, and it does work when I have to use it, but my consciousness has changed around this topic and I don't need to rely on it anymore. Learning it has changed me at some deep, subconscious level. To me, this hints at a supportive mechanism inside us that takes over once we master a new technique. I think it is quite hopeful to consider this somewhat mysterious process that can take place inside of us when we learn something new and practice it.

Another thing I've noticed is that although I feel uncomfortable when I'm holding my breath, I've never felt like I was close to passing out during breath holding. The feeling I have is more like the one I get after an intense swim set in a workout. Or a sprint run where I get out of breath.

I feel like I should remind you again that I'm not a doctor. Nor am I suggesting that this technique will work for everyone. In fact, if you decide to try the breath-holding technique, please consult with your doctor before doing so. Especially if you have a heart condition, asthma, are a smoker, have lung disease, or have other medical conditions, then I wouldn't try it.

You should check with your doctor first. What I do know for sure is that I'm happy I tried it. Breath holding helped change my life.

Breath-holding Q&A

The following are some common questions that people have around the breath-holding technique, including some that came up in a recent webinar I co-led on the topic.

What goes through your head when trying breath holding?

At the beginning of the process of using the breath-holding technique, what goes through my head now is mostly focusing on my breathing. I like to take a long, slow breath out, then hold it. I do have a lot of the same negative thoughts enter my head that I used to . . . but I just don't pay much attention to them anymore. I don't give the negative thoughts any energy to be real. I breathe out until a point at which I start holding my breath. Then I don't really think of much else. I focus on my breath and wait until I start to feel that gasp reflex. At that point my body wants air so much that it is impossible for me to think of anything else aside from breathing.

If you're not a swimmer (or other type of athlete), will this work for me?

Yes, it can. I know others who are not swimmers or athletes who have successfully used the breath-holding technique.

Do you have to practice? If so, how?

I and others who have mastered this technique have found that practice is not necessary. Once it worked for me, it worked almost every time I tried it. That said, I enjoy the feeling of being able to pee in public, especially in difficult situations. So I practice for fun, not because I have to in order for the technique to be effective.

How long does it take to work?

This varies from person to person. For some people it can take from 30 to 60 seconds.[11] Initially it took me somewhere between 60 to 90 seconds. Soon after I did it a few times, it took me much less time, usually under a minute.

---

[11] Soifer, S., *Zgourides*, G. D., Himle, J., & O'Brien, N. (2020). *The Secret Social Phobia: Shy bladder syndrome (paruresis): Second Edition.* International Paruresis Association, Inc., 134-136.

Is it ok to start holding your breath before you enter the bathroom?

I have not tried this, but it could be an effective strategy. It might be worth safely experimenting with.

Why does this work for some people and not others?

I'm not sure. In talking with many people who have tried it and for whom it didn't work, the consistent theme I hear is that it was too "uncomfortable." As I mentioned above there is a fear factor involved in the brain when a person holds their breath. It can be difficult to override this fear to the point of being able to release the sphincter muscle. For me, it was more uncomfortable not to be able to pee in public than it was to hold my breath beyond what was comfortable.

19.

Primary Paruresis Recovery Resources, Tips & Techniques

What I've learned in my own personal recovery from primary paruresis is that there are many types of techniques, tips and treatments that have been shown to help me and others improve and even recover. I've tried several different tips and techniques, including breath holding and graduated exposure, which were both life-changing for me. I've explained my experience using these techniques throughout this book.

I wrote this chapter to help point you to the most prominent resources, tips, techniques and treatments that I have learned about through researching the International Paruresis Association (IPA) website, along with attending two and co-facilitating one Shy Bladder Workshop. I can't speak to each technique and treatment's effectiveness personally, as I have not tried them all, but I will list resources that will help you learn more about each, and you can decide for yourself if it makes sense to try them. I also recommend visiting the IPA website and reading the book *The Secret Social*

Phobia: Shy Blader Syndrome (Paruresis). Both contain information about numerous therapies and techniques to treat shy bladder syndrome, several of which are not mentioned here, and also list resources where you can find additional information.

Reading *The Secret Social Phobia* was one of the first things I did in my own recovery journey, and I highly recommend it.

Talking with your doctor and/or urologist

As you embark on, or continue, your journey to recover from paruresis, the first thing I'd suggest is to talk with your doctor or urologist. This is to make sure that your challenge of not being able to urinate isn't because of a physical/medical problem. Today more and more doctors and urologists are familiar with paruresis, or know it as shy bladder syndrome, and can provide you with medical advice. I have spoken to my doctors in the past about my condition, but they were not concerned because I did not have any physical problems, such as an enlarged prostate.

Graduated Exposure

The basic premise of this approach involves jumping right in to do what is fearful and causing you anxiety, doing it gradually, and doing it often. I cover my experiences with this technique in detail in the chapters "In-Person Workshop" and "What Happens in Vegas." My experience at the convention center was one of graduated exposure therapy that I did by myself.

You can also read much more about the graduated exposure technique, including the steps to practice it on your own, in the book *The Secret Social Phobia: Shy Blader Syndrome (Paruresis)*.

Pee-Practice

In order for graduated exposure to work, it needs to be practiced, both during the graduated exposure training as well as afterwards. This might sound odd—practicing to pee? But for many people who have learned and continue to use graduated exposure as a recovery technique, practicing urinating in public is crucial to their recovery. As a competitive swimmer and lifelong athlete, I understand the value of practice for maintaining fitness, getting into competitive shape, and performing at a high level.

For many, practicing helps normalize the experience of urinating in public. By regularly putting themselves in situations that once seemed uncomfortable, they retrain their minds to see these situations differently. I've found that while practicing regularly helps many people, my recent insight has shown me that I don't actually *need* to practice anymore. Something shifted within me that has shifted the way I experience my shy bladder. Situations that I once considered hard or impossible, like peeing at a urinal, are no longer difficult for me. However, I still find practicing fun, so I do it anyway.

I've even gamified the practice to make it enjoyable. Instead of thinking, "I should go to the bathroom before I leave the house," I now ask myself, "What bathrooms can I find out in the world to challenge me today?" This new mindset encourages me to face more challenging situations.

I've found public rest areas are great practice areas. They are usually poorly designed for people with shy bladders. There's one nearby with no dividers between the urinals. It's been a great place to practice. Also, there are retail outlets with restaurants nearby as well. That area is great due to the high tourist traffic and general busyness of the restrooms.

Another great practice area is at large shopping malls, retail stores, and busy restaurants/bars. There's a pizza place near where I live that has urinals designed so the ceramic goes all the way to the floor. It's like you're peeing on the wall and the ground. It's modeled after urinals at places like Fenway Park, where they encourage you to pee freely (as long as you are able to). I stopped in there recently to give it a try, because it has always been a challenge for me. Interestingly, I found that I still had a hard time going. There was a man standing nearby, and I approached the other available urinal with a little nervousness and what I thought was a full bladder. But I couldn't go! As we learned at our workshop and support groups, this is nothing but a "misfire." I was able to urinate after the man left the bathroom and it was empty. Which is still a win for me, because the old me would have been worried that someone else was going to walk in.

I like to practice as often as I can, although I work from home and don't always make it to a public place every day. Recently I met up with a "pee buddy" from my Boston Workshop, who also lives in Maine. We met for coffee and then had a practice session at a nearby coffee shop that's conveniently located in a business with a great practice bathroom—because it has several urinals with divider walls, and the location has a good amount of foot traffic. The chances of someone else being in the bathroom are pretty high there.

Ultimately, while I don't feel the need to practice as much due to my insights about the nature of thought and reality, I continue to do so because I find it enjoyable and it keeps me engaged in my recovery journey.

Retraining Your Bladder

Another important lesson I learned attending workshops is the significance of waiting until my bladder is full before attempting to urinate. The bladder is a complex organ, with a lot going on structurally. One of the important steps to being able to urinate, is having a full bladder. Too often people who have paruresis will go when they feel it's "safe" to do so (myself included for most of my life). This often means that we will try and go at home before we leave the house, to avoid any uncertain bathroom situations. Or in my case, for example, I always tried to use a "safe" hotel bathroom at the airport, whether I really need to go or not, and then avoid drinking for the rest of my travel. I was operating out of a state of fear, thinking ahead to all of the ways my day could go wrong if I couldn't find a bathroom that I could pee in.

Over time, and for me this was decades, our bladder never really learns to go in public when the sense of urgency is great. We also never learn what it feels like to have a full bladder.

So we often go when we have a mild urge (say a 4 or a 5 on a 1-10 scale), when really it can be helpful to wait a little longer. If we are always trying to go based on outside factors involving safe bathrooms, we are interfering with the normal rhythm of this bodily process. In fact, we're overthinking and over-preparing, and this can put even more mental pressure on us.

I now typically wait until I reach a higher level of urgency (7 or 8). This adjustment has been uncomfortable but significantly improved my ability to urinate in public restrooms. Now when I enter a public restroom, I really have to go, and my body knows that. My ability to void is much greater since I've retrained my bladder.

The Breath-Holding Technique

This technique I learned about through researching the IPA website. I was inspired to try it after watching a video interview between the IPA Executive Director, Tim Pyle, and David Kliss, who is an IPA board member and support group leader.[12] Dave's life was changed forever when he learned the breath-hold technique. He explained the mechanics around how it works in the video, and I decided to try it, which changed my life forever. I write extensively about this technique in the chapter entitled "Breath Holding."[13]

Self-Catheterization

Urinary catheterization is the act of inserting small rubber or plastic tubes through the urethra into the bladder. This is the technique you may be familiar with that is used in hospitals for patients who can't get out of bed. The nice thing about this technique is that once you learn how to do it, it is nearly 100% reliable.

I've never tried this, although many people use this procedure to void in situations that they are unable to otherwise, such as on airplanes. This is a technique that you should meet with your urologist to discuss and learn how to do it safely.

Stadium Pal

During one of the workshops I attended, I learned about a

---

[12] https://paruresis.org/breath-hold/

[13] Dave's email sign-off is "Feel the Flow." This fact, combined with my mastering of the breath-hold technique, together form the inspiration for the title of this book.

type of catheter called a Stadium Pal, or also known as a condom catheter. The device was originally created for sporting event attendees so they could drink beer and relieve themselves while never having to leave their seat. This ensured they didn't have to wait in long lines or miss any of the sporting event. Many people who have paruresis have found comfort in having the stadium pal as a backup plan or even a first option during travel, such as on airplanes. It's a device that works similarly to a regular catheter, but the major difference is that, for men, there is a condom that you attach to your penis, which leads to a tube and empties into a plastic reservoir you attach to your leg. IPA president Dan Rocker has a video on the IPA website where you can learn more about how to use this device, and how easy and unnoticeable it is.[14]

Drug Treatments

I have not tried any drugs to help me with my paruresis. However, according to the IPA's website there are drugs that can help people suffering from paruresis. As there are two components to paruresis, a physical component and a psychological component, there are different drugs that may help with either or both. Drugs that help relieve anxiety and fear may help with the psychological part of the condition. Drugs that affect the bladder or sphincter muscles may help with the physical part of the condition, by relaxing those areas. There are also drugs to avoid.

As with everything else in this book, I recommend doing your own research and talking with your doctor before deciding if drugs are the right approach for you.

---

[14] https://paruresis.org/stadium-pal-gal/

Psychologists, other licensed therapists, or trained coaches

There are some psychologists, licensed therapists, and trained coaches who are specialists in working with people who suffer from Shy Bladder Syndrome. Many who are trained and experienced working with people who suffer from paruresis appear in the Shy Bladder Center directory.[15] Some of these professionals specialize in Cognitive Behavioral Therapy, which is a therapy that has been shown to help people who have this condition. I have been active as a Shy Bladder Center coach since July of 2024, and I hope the number of active coaches in this area increases.

Support Groups

One of the first activities I participated in during my recovery from paruresis was the virtual support group I wrote about earlier. It was an amazing experience for me, and it was the first time I told my story of living with shy bladder to anyone.

The IPA support groups[16] are led by people who have experience attending or leading workshops, and have either recovered from or are on their own journey of recovery from paruresis. The men and women who attend the workshops are all sufferers, and all have different experiences. The support group sessions start off by allowing everyone to tell their story, if they wish. For many people this is the first time that they've told their story to anyone else. As I mentioned, I found it to be very healing, as well as to hear other people's stories. I realized how I was not broken, and it helped to "normalize" my shy bladder. The leaders

---

[15] https://paruresis.org/sbc-therapists/
[16] https://paruresis.org/shy-bladder-support-groups/

may share some tips during the meeting, but mostly it's a venue for people to be able to share their story and hear other people's stories.

Some cities and states have local, in-person support groups. Part of the meeting in the in-person groups involves a practice session, which works in the same way that workshop practice sessions operate. I created a support group in the state of Maine, and you can reach out to me if you live in the Portland area to find out more.

20.

You Are Perfect

I've come to realize during my journey with shy bladder that we are all perfect. You, me, everyone is perfect the way we are. We are whole, happy, pure love, contented . . . We are perfection—aside from our thinking in the moment, which isn't perfect or imperfect; it just *is*.

We all have a truly amazing capacity to heal, to overcome adversity, to persevere. There is nothing to do about it really. It's part of our design.

The power of thought provides every human being the gift of being able to create our reality, whatever that reality is to us in the moment. And the way we are designed, we feel those thoughts through our senses. Often this comes with a physical sensation. I feel embarrassed, my cheeks get red, I feel warmer; I might even get lightheaded.

For decades I thought I was broken. I thought that my inability to void in a public situation meant that I was less than others. I was ashamed of myself. I judged myself for being unable to do something that most people found it natural and easy to do.

There were times where I wanted to physically hurt myself because of the negative thoughts I believed about myself. And there were times where I actually did do this—in ways like digging my nails into my arm or biting my lip out of frustration for not being able to pee when I really had to.

Today I realize that I am human, and my essence is perfection. There is nowhere I need to be or visit, no status I need to attain to be happy. I am designed perfectly, and my body has an amazing capacity to heal itself. Upon reflection I realize that I've healed from Lyme disease, from frozen shoulder, from broken bones, cuts, pulled muscles . . . I've healed from depression, and other negative thinking habits. I've changed bad habitual thinking around drinking alcohol, chewing tobacco, eating unhealthy food, and have created new, healthier thinking.

I've experienced personal change I never thought possible. Sometimes our bodies can heal all on their own, and sometimes we need some support to help us.

YOU have this magic healing power within you as well. It is part of your essence.

Whatever challenges you're facing, or think you're facing, you have the ability to heal.

You are perfect, just the way you are.

We are all connected and part of the universal intelligent energy that powers every living thing.

21.

Conclusion

I wrote this book to help people who are suffering realize that there is hope.

In my case I was suffering from a severe anxiety disorder called paruresis, which I had lived with for over fifty years. It controlled my life, my decisions, my actions. I didn't think I could be cured. A small piece of me believed there was hope. But it was a really small piece.

One day I had had enough and released everything to the Universe. And two months later I considered myself mostly recovered from this fifty-year anxiety disorder.

I've blogged about my experience and have told dozens of people about it. I've been interviewed on global podcasts. And I've written this book. I have started a local paruresis support group, and have also become a Shy Bladder Center Coach, facilitating IPA Workshops and working with people one-on-one.

I have experienced that the Universe is magical. There is something bigger than us that is behind everything we create. I've found that by quieting my thinking and operating from a clearer mind, there are answers waiting. For my shy bladder, there was a cure. I just had to quiet my mind to "find" it.

I've also realized that the negative stories I've been telling myself about my urinating or not in the bathroom are all made up. Innocent, yet still made up. The layers upon layers of thinking from which they arise are just that: thinking. As I started to understand this, my thinking calmed down and I didn't give nearly as much attention to those negative thoughts. Now I actually look forward to using public restrooms. I've turned it into a game, of sorts. My reality has changed.

My wish for you is that the same thing will happen in your own life.

At the very least I hope my story might help you to discover your own unique way forward, and to see your own innocence, perfection and potential for transformation.

There is hope for you, not just related to shy bladder but for any other challenge you're facing. For you personally, and for anyone you care about.

Appendices

Appendix I

The Three Principles of Mind, Consciousness and Thought

In the chapter "We Live in an Inside-Out Reality," I mentioned that one of the things that has helped me overcome paruresis is my deep understanding that our experience of life comes from the inside-out. I wrote this chapter to help the reader explore the origins of the psychological principles behind this understanding. As I wrote in that earlier chapter, it is not necessary to study or understand these principles to recover from paruresis. But I do believe that my grounding in this understanding helped *me*, at least, overcome my decades-long battle with my shy bladder.

Sydney "Syd" Banks was a Scottish welder living on an island near Vancouver, British Columbia. In the early 1970s he had an enlightenment experience—that it seems only a few people throughout history have had, where they see a spiritual truth that can't be unseen. This in turn leads them to not being able to look at life in the same way ever again.

In Syd's case, his enlightenment experience was a vision that completely changed the way he saw the universe. Once he experienced this vision, he changed so much that his friends barely recognized him in terms of the man he had been. Soon after he was inspired to leave his welding job and share what he discovered with the world, which he proceeded to do over the next several decades until his death in 2009.

What Syd discovered was that there are three underlying psychological principles behind how we operate as human beings. I will share these here, with the caveat that Syd often encouraged people to be patient with him in his talks, because he was trying to explain the unexplainable. He was, he said, using words to explain a spiritual understanding. So, if the words you're reading here don't make sense, that's okay. I recommend reflecting on what comes to mind for you in your life as you read this.

By Syd's definition, principles mean universal laws, of the same caliber as the law of gravity. And, like gravity, these laws are invisible, but they certainly exist, whether we believe in them or not. These principles have come to be known as "The Three Principles of Mind, Consciousness, and Thought." Or just "The Three Principles." I'll define them below, as I have come to understand them.

The Three Principles underlie all human experience and help explain our experience of life.

- **Mind** is the intelligent energy behind all things. Mind is behind what grows an acorn into a tree. Mind is behind what heals a cut on your hand. Mind is behind the new idea that pops into your head that appears to be "out of the blue." Mind is the formless, intelligent energy behind all human experience and creation.

- **Consciousness** is our ability as human beings to be *aware* of our experience. That awareness is constant, but it seems fluid because of thought. It is Consciousness that "gives life" to thoughts and allows us to feel them.

- **Thought** is a tool we use to create our reality. We have thousands of thoughts a day, yet only make a small number of them "real." This tool of thought is neutral. But via thought we create our experience moment to moment by assigning meaning to certain thoughts. We have an amazing gift to use this tool of thought however we want to in life.

Syd taught that we are conditioned from an early age to believe that our experiences are coming from outside ourselves. This leads to thinking like, "That person made me feel bad when they were mean to me," "I'd be happy if only I didn't have to go to work," or "Everything would be fine if my son would just behave." You can fill in the blanks with your own thoughts, I'm sure.

What Syd shared, and what the Three Principles point to, is the fact that our experiences are 100 percent created from within. A person might be mean to me, but how I think about that situation is what shapes how I feel about it. That is, if someone is mean to me and I think, "That's not fair!" then this is a thought that I'm believing in that moment. I am making that thought real to me, because of what I am believing to be true. I am giving that thought energy and bringing it to life. Or I could choose one hundred, one thousand, one million different thoughts to believe about it. "They must be having a bad day," "They must not like me," "Yeah, I deserved that," "What a jerk."

The Three Principles are not a "how-to" technique or strategy. They simply describe an understanding of how we operate as human beings. The "What's behind it all?" of life. When we start to live from the understanding that our thinking, and our reaction to it, creates our experience of reality, it becomes easier not to get caught up in the whirlwind of thought. This leads to a deeper sense of inner calm, clearer thinking, and a more peaceful experience of life.

I've come to realize that the stories we tell ourselves and the meaning we give to those stories varies from moment to moment. We, as the thinkers, can decide the meaning we assign our thinking. Sometimes our thinking is negative, sometimes it's positive—depending on the meaning we make up about it in the moment. Furthermore, that meaning can change depending on our mood. What seems like a negative thought in a low mood, might take a positive spin when we're in a better mood. When we're in a particularly good mood we might even laugh at how strange life can be when we can't accomplish something we can normally do—such as when, for some reason, I can't pee even in a place where I've gone before. When such a thing happens, I could give it the meaning that something's gone wrong and I'm going to have to struggle to make sure I can go next time. Or I can simply try again later.

The coolest thing about the "practice" of the Three Principles is that there is absolutely nothing to do about any of it—other than to notice our thinking. Positive or negative thinking is not intrinsically good or bad; it just is. It's completely neutral until we make meaning about it. And the act of noticing it, of being aware of our thinking—the principle of Consciousness—eventually brings us back to a neutral state. That is, when we stop fighting our "cluttered" and stressful thinking and allow it to simply be, our mind eventually calms itself.

And this is where the magic happens. In this neutral space, unclouded by overthinking, we are open to new thoughts—which come through to us via the Universal Mind.

I've shared here the fundamental understanding of the Three Principles. As I mentioned in the chapter "My Major Insight," if you feel inspired, play with these concepts rather than seeing them as something you have to study to "get." If they don't "click" with you, that's fine. I'm sharing them simply because of the impact they've had on my life, in the hope that they may also support you in some way in your own life. Whether we understand it or not, the Three Principles help explain our thought-created reality, however awful or wonderful that reality seems to be. Just like gravity helps explain why we fall when we lose our balance, or how it works to our advantage for a hole-in-one.

Appendix II

The Coaching Experience

As a coach, I not only support people who are experiencing shy bladder syndrome, but other types of anxiety-related issues as well, such as stress, overwhelm, OCD, insecurity, and fearful thoughts. People often come to me feeling stuck and not knowing what to do, just as I have myself felt in the past. The thinking that they have used up to this point has not helped them, and they typically feel trapped in their thought patterns. They've tried many ways to relieve their suffering, but nothing seems to help for long.

When I coach, my goal is to be fully present with the human being sitting across from me. We are all connected—energetically, spiritually—in an invisible way to the source that Sydney Banks described as Mind, and we can probably all think of experiences where we've experienced this connection in a tangible way. Like when you're thinking of your daughter and she calls you in the next minute. Or you think to call your best friend, and they tell you they were just thinking of you. In athletics you've probably seen a professional athlete being interviewed about their amazing game or match. They're asked, "How did you do it?" and the athlete's response is "I don't know, I was just in the zone." That zone is the space within us where we can "sync" with ourselves in a profound way.

It's also the space we can drop into when we are being fully present with another human being. By showing up this way we can help ourselves and others experience insights, see new ideas and understand that they don't need anything "out there" to help them feel better. We all have wisdom and wellbeing built into us. I see my primary job as helping my clients to realize a different way of thinking about things and to experience new thoughts or feelings about whatever problem they think they have going on.

I ask questions to help point people back to their inner wisdom and operate from a clear state of mind. I let my intuition guide me rather than having a pre-formulated list of questions to ask. I do my best to be fully present and in full service to the other person, without a specific agenda.

In my own experience of being coached, it has not been the specific question a coach has asked me that's led to my own insights so much as the timing of the question in the moment that's made me stop, reflect, and go inside myself for the answer. It was my coach's ability to hear what I was saying "between the words"—and their being in touch with their own wisdom—that prompted them to ask the question in the first place.

Group Exercise

I sometimes use the following exercise in my group workshops to help people get out of their intellect and really see the role of thought in their lives, in particular how we are often weighed down by thought and unable to see clearly.

We all have at least twenty to thirty things we are juggling in our mind at any one time. We are expected to be great multi-taskers. But sometimes having all of this stuff on our mind can create situations we weren't expecting.

Think of a time you had twenty things on your mind, and you did something that, looking back on it, was funny. Here's an example I use to lead the discussion: the other day I was making coffee; I hit the start button and walked away. All of a sudden, I heard a dripping noise that didn't sound normal. I went to the coffee pot to check on it and I saw water going everywhere: on the counter, on the floor . . . I'd had so much on my mind that I had forgotten to put the carafe in the machine.

Group Reflection

When I ask the group to share their stories, the floodgates start to open. I've heard stories ranging from, "I missed the highway exit that I take every day to get to work" to "I spent ten minutes looking for my car keys, which when I slowed down I found in my pocket" to "I couldn't find my sunglasses, which were already on my head" to "I ended up at checkout at the grocery store with my cart half-full of my own groceries, and half-full of someone else's."

After everyone shares their story of doing something funny because they had so much on their mind, we generally share a great teaching moment.

Follow-up Questions

Below I share some of the questions and invitations to reflect that I might use during this exercise (and which I might also ask in a one-on-one coaching session, if it seems appropriate). Feel free to consider where the question applies in your life:

How often do you spend thinking about the past?

Reflection: There is nothing wrong with this; we all do it. But when we are thinking of the past, know that *our past* is the experience we are living in that moment, right then. We are carrying these thoughts with us and keeping the past alive. And it's hard to be present when we are focused on the past.

How often do you spend thinking about the future?

Reflection: this reflection is similar to the one above, in that when we think in the future we are also experiencing that future, which can include all of our worries and fears about it.

Where do you think the feeling of overwhelm comes from? Worry? Anxious thinking?

Reflection: When we have too much thinking going on, it can seem like we're carrying a heavy weight. This thought metaphorically weighs us down and causes us to feel overwhelm, worry, anxiety, and so on.

Where else in our lives is our busy thinking clouding our judgement?

Reflection: Consider how operating from a busy mind or a clear mind impacts our lives in other areas.

When we are trying really hard to figure something out, when do we usually find the answers—when we're in a busy or a clear mind?

Reflection: Operating from a clear mind is not a place to "get to."

It's our natural state.

Where does peace of mind really come from? Where in your life have you faced a big challenge and somehow made it through?

Reflection: Does thinking about this question give you any insights into how we all are connected to a universal, intelligent energy?

I've written earlier about how my life has been positively impacted by The Three Principles. Much of that impact came to me via coaching sessions. Two of the most impactful insights I have had by being coached are:

- My reality is different than every other human being—we are all creating our own, unique experiences via the gift of thought.

- My thinking—not my external circumstances—completely, 100 percent, creates my reality in the moment.

The two client examples I share below point to other people I have coached who have had these same insights.

Two Different Experiences

Here's an example of a recent coaching conversation in which I asked the following:

Me: "Where in your life have you and a friend both done essentially the same thing but each had a completely difference experience?"

Client: "My husband and I went on a trip, where we had to take a flight to get to our destination. Both of us were on the same flight, sitting next to each other. I was relaxed. I watched a movie, read a book and was having a wonderful experience. It was the first time I've let myself relax for a few hours with nothing on my mind. It was a pleasant experience, and I really enjoyed flying, so I also really had fun. Especially because the plane was a Boeing 757, and it's my favorite commercial plane to fly in. My husband, however, had a very different experience. He's afraid of flying and thinks of all of the worst case "what if" scenarios, and then gets anxious about the flight. He grabs my hand and squeezes it pretty hard (which is okay with me) during takeoff and also when there is turbulence. I can tell he can't concentrate on doing anything for any length of time, such as watching a movie, because he can't focus. Which means he interrupts my movie time quite often during the flight. So we were both on the same plane but had very different experiences."

Our Thoughts Create Our Reality (not our circumstances)

One particular client story that stands out to me involves my work with Alicia (I've changed her name and some details to protect her privacy). When I first started meeting with her, she was in a low mood. She was upset and frustrated about her coworkers. She felt she was being treated unfairly and that her work had no meaning. She felt unvalued as an employee.

Her frustration was bleeding over into her personal life as well. She was an athlete, and although she enjoyed working out at the gym, she hadn't been there in weeks. She would work and then head home, feeling too tired to do anything else. Weekends were spent thinking about work, and she really didn't enjoy herself. She also was having trouble connecting with people and making friends.

Through our work together I pointed out to Alica how her thoughts were creating her reality, moment to moment, and that she actually had everything she needed inside of her to feel great, to be okay and to live life to the fullest. Over time, she started to see for herself how her thoughts were causing her to believe that her stress was due to circumstances outside of her. Alicia told me that she was spending more time noticing the power of her thoughts. Noticing that her thinking was causing her to create her reality, which seemed real in the moment, but which was created by her thinking. She started paying less attention to her negative thoughts and more attention to the optimistic thoughts that gave her a good feeling. As she started to take ownership of her thinking and realize that thoughts are temporary and only come alive when we give attention to them, her stress began to melt away.

In fact, Alica started to flourish in her job. She quickly received a promotion and engaged with her coworkers and customers more. She began exercising again, and making new friends.

Today, Alicia is a valued member of the team at her business. Her boss often goes to her for ideas, and she also proactively brings them to management. She loves her job and her customers. She tells me how customers are coming back again and again because of how much they love the service they receive.

Although not every day is sunshine and roses—all of us can slip back into habitual, negative thinking—she is thankful that she understands what is behind it all. Her only problem today is that she says she has become a bit of a local celebrity and it's hard for her to go out without being recognized by her customers.

Additional Resources

Websites:

International Paruresis Association Website:
https://paruresis.org

Videos:

Graduated Exposure Video:
https://youtu.be/f7XVP38RMrY?si=18KPG7D9dQpsGWq2

Breath-holding Technique Video:
https://youtu.be/-aqXh2IXbdM?si=1LqFhj1fHsPbaruX

Sydney Banks' Long Beach Lectures:
https://sydbanks.com/longbeach/

Books:

The Secret Social Phobia: Shy Bladder Syndrome (Paruresis): The definitive book on shy bladder syndrome: Second Edition, by S. Soifer, G. Zgourides, J. Himle, & N. O'Brien (2020)

The Missing Link, by Sydney Banks (2021)

Second Chance, by Sydney Banks (2021)

The Inside-Out Revolution: The Only Thing You Need to Know to Change Your Life Forever, by Michael Neill (2013)

Breath: The New Science of a Lost Art, by James Nestor (2020)

Acknowledgments

I have many people who helped inspire me to begin this project and see it to publication. I never imagined I'd ever write a book. It's amazing what insight and inspiration can accomplish. I would like to thank:

- My daughters, Ellie and Laurel, and my wife Susan, for being the first proofreaders of this book, and for being supportive of this project. Your feedback and ongoing encouragement were invaluable to me. I love you.

- Cathy Casey – your coaching, mentorship, guidance, and friendship have been life-changing. Spending time with you over the last few years has been amazing. I value your ability to help me see the "real me" and gain clarity and an overall sense of well-being. And, of course, thank you for being an early reader of my book and for providing me with some great suggestions.

- Rick Ruppenthal and Marlene Cameron – thanks for playing the Service Game with me. I always look forward to our weekly sessions, and I know that somewhere along the way our discussions gave me insight to want to start (and finish) this project. I'm so grateful for you taking the time to read early drafts of my book, which helped me create what it is today.

- Aila Hale – I am so grateful to you for your coaching support, and also for introducing me to Chris Nelson. You continuously teach me new ways to serve others. I am thrilled that I am in your orbit. I am also grateful for you reading early versions of my book and encouraging me to move forward with this project.

- Chris Nelson, my editor, whose writing and editing skills helped me turn my ideas into a real book. Your ability to help me organize my ideas into an order that makes sense for the reader helped give me the confidence to publish this book. Your editing and coaching have been invaluable, and I am forever grateful that you helped me organize my thoughts into a published book. You are a wonderful human being and it's been fun working with you.

- Tim Pyle – thank you for literally changing my life. I had only dreamed of overcoming my shy bladder, and you helped point me in a direction to recover from my decades-long phobia. Thank you for your friendship, and for writing the amazing foreward to this book.

- Steve Soifer – thank you for helping me overcome my paruresis. Reading your book was one of the very first things I did. I appreciate the research you do and your contributions in multiple ways, such as sharing helpful content in your book, your online videos, and in leading the workshop that I attended in Boston. I also learned a lot from you during our time co-facilitating the IPA workshop in Detroit. And, of course, I greatly appreciate you taking the time to read and provide your valuable feedback for this book.

Acknowledgments

- Dan Rocker – thank you for your contagious enthusiasm in helping demonstrate to me that "nobody really cares" what I'm doing in the bathroom. Your "crazy person" demonstration of this at the mall bathroom in Natick during our Boston IPA workshop will always stick with me. You inspire me with your dedication to serving and supporting this community. Thanks as well for taking time to be an early reader of this book.

- David Kliss – thank you for having the courage to film the breath holding interview with Tim Pyle and posting it on the IPA website. That video literally changed my life… which led to my writing this book. The virtual support groups that you lead are where I first got the nerve to share my story with others. Due to your openness and sharing, I am definitely "feeling the flow" today. And I am grateful for you for being an early reader of my book.

- Steven Jackson – thank you for inviting us all to participate in your documentary at the Boston IPA Workshop. Little did I know that I would be a "star" in your amazing film, which I know will be helpful to so many people. The conversations we had during the filming—both on- and offscreen were thought-provoking. I appreciate your friendship and your willingness to be an early reader of my book.

- Thank you to all of the additional early readers of my book, including Melissa Ford, Bonnie Jarvis, Michael Lehrman, Dr. Holly Brown, Steven Weinraub and others (I'm sorry if I've left anyone off!). I am super grateful for your time, effort and support. Your feedback and encouragement have been the wind in my sails to complete this project.

- Lastly, thank you to the IPA leadership, volunteers, and members. I feel so fortunate that I finally found this caring organization and am now part of the amazing paruresis community.

Love to you all,

Mike

About the Author

Michael Hurd is a life and business coach, as well as a coach with the International Paruresis Association's Shy Bladder Center and a member of its Board of Directors. He helps people navigate anxiety, stress, overwhelm, and invisible challenges, supporting them in finding clarity, confidence, and peace of mind.

Michael lives on the coast of Maine with his wife of thirty-three years and their rescue cat, Lily. He is a competitive swimmer, U.S. Masters swim coach, adult learn-to-swim instructor, and high school swim official. His love of the water and belief in the human capacity for resilience are at the heart of everything he does.

Work With Mike

If something in this book resonated with you—if you're living with shy bladder syndrome, facing invisible struggles, or simply looking for a new way forward—I'd love to connect.

I work with people around the world through one-on-one coaching, group programs, and speaking. My approach is personal, practical, and rooted in the understanding that real change begins from the inside out.

Whether you're navigating anxiety, overwhelm, or a turning point in your life or work, you don't have to figure it out alone.

Learn more or schedule a complimentary conversation at:

https://www.michaelrhurd.com/

www.ingramcontent.com/pod-product-compliance
Lightning Source LLC
Chambersburg PA
CBHW071257130626
46556CB00003B/1348